Pottery Book for Beginners

An Instruction Guide for Potters to Sculpt Wheel Thrown and Handbuilding Ceramic Projects With Tips, Techniques and Pottery Tools Included

By

Wade Marsh

Copyright © 2021 – Wade Marsh
All rights reserved

No part of this publication may be reproduced, distributed, or transmitted in any form or by any means, including photocopying, recording, or other electronic or mechanical methods, without the prior written permission of the publisher, except in the case of brief quotations embodied in reviews and certain other non-commercial uses permitted by copyright law.

Disclaimer

This publication is designed to provide competent and reliable information regarding the subject matter covered. However, the views expressed in this publication are those of the author alone, and should not be taken as expert instruction or professional advice. The reader is responsible for his or her own actions.

The author hereby disclaims any responsibility or liability whatsoever that is incurred from the use or application of the contents of this publication by the purchaser or reader. The purchaser or reader is hereby responsible for his or her own actions.

Table of Contents

Introduction 7

Chapter 1 8

Fundamentals of Pottery Making 8

    What is Pottery? 8

    Understanding Handbuilding Pottery 10

    History of Pottery Making 11

    Composition of Pottery 14

    Health Benefits of Pottery 17

Chapter 2 21

Glossary of Pottery Making Terms 21

Chapter 3 35

Pottery Making Tips and Tricks 35

Chapter 4 38

Pottery Making Process 38

    Clay Preparation 38

Wedging 39

Forming 40

Drying 41

Leather Hard 42

Greenware 42

Bisque Firing 43

Glazing 45

Glaze Firing 46

Overglaze Firing 47

Chapter 5 50

Getting Started With Pottery Making 50

Basic Tools, Supplies, and Equipment 50

    Wedging Board/Workbench 51
    Aprons and Towels 52
    Chamois 53
    Potter's Needles 54
    Cut-Off Wires 54
    Fettling Knives 55
    Ribs and Scrapers 56
    Loop, Wire, and Ribbons 58

    Wooden Modeling Tools 58
    Sponges 59
    Potter's Calipers 60
    Rolling Pin 60
    Pottery Clay 61
    Glaze and Other Decorating Materials 63
    Pottery Wheel 64
    Kiln 66
Setting Up Your Pottery Making Workspace 67

Safety Guidelines For Pottery Making 78

Pottery Forming Techniques 83

    Slab Pots 83
    Pinch Pots 84
    Coil Pots 85
    Wheel-Thrown Pottery 87
    Slip Cast 88

Chapter 6 89

Pottery Making Project Ideas 89

Handbuilt Coil Pot 89

Handbuilt Pinch Pot Hedgehog 98

Handbuilt Slab Water Font 105

Wheel Thrown Hookah Head 118

Pottery Clay Tray 132

Wheel Thrown Mug... 137

Handbuilt Slab Shoe 147

Wheel Thrown Chicken Coop Waterer 160

Wheel Thrown Pottery Bowl.. 175

Handbuilt Clay Starfish Box... 185

Chapter 7 200

Common Pottery Making Mistakes To Avoid..................... 200

Chapter 8 208

Pottery Questions To Ask Before Starting Out.................... 208

Introduction

Pottery, a craft introduced far back, is responsible for most of the ceramics and other earthenware projects that we use today. It is a process by which clay is molded either by hand or wheel-thrown to produce different pieces of pottery crafts such as cups, plates, mugs, vases, and many more. To make these pottery crafts, several types of tools, supplies and equipment are employed, and so, you would need a proper guide as encapsulated in this book to put you through how they work and their usage. Also discussed in the pages of this book are the processes involved in making pottery projects and the different pottery techniques you can employ to make awesome pottery projects. That is why this book, **Pottery Book for Beginners**, was written to take you by the hand and to guide you on your journey from being a novice to becoming an experienced potter in the art of pottery-making.

Now, let's delve into the art of pottery making, shall we?

Chapter 1

Fundamentals of Pottery Making

Pottery making is one of the commonest and easiest arts that you can delve into as an artist. It requires very few and relatively cheap materials and can serve to make a lot of money. Here, we will be studying the fundamentals guiding the art of pottery making and the basic things you need to know as a beginner.

What is Pottery?

Pottery is the finished work of clay molding. It is usually done through molding, drying, firing—either with a glaze or finish—and other detailed techniques to form a container or another item. The principal material used in the art of pottery is clay, and clay can be obtained from the earth naturally.

Clay is a kind of soil that is formed from the decomposition of rocks within the soil for several years. The decomposition of the rocks is a process that is activated when water repeatedly runs across the surfaces and then causes them to get eroded gradually.

Eroding usually weakens the forces at the uppermost layer, which breaks down the whole entity.

Now, the term 'clay' is entirely different from 'clay bodies.' The latter is a term that describes a lump of clay that contains elements that improve the qualities of clay. This way, when the clay body is taken through the firing or any other structural process, it comes out with a unique property from the other clay bodies.

The term 'clay bodies' comes into play in pottery since that is what is used, not the normal and unrefined kind of clay. The clay body can form the final product when it is worked on, e.g., cups, mugs, etc. The working can be done with the hands of a potter or with the aid of a throwing wheel, which is powered electrically.

Other tools aid in replicating the models or designs used in crafting out the original pieces of a clay project. But then, usually, the clay is set in shaped molds and then dried. Once it is dried, it is then cut up and stamped at different parts.

To also get the clay set permanently in the size in which it is shaped, the process of having it fired comes out as another very crucial step. Here, the molded clay project is placed in a kiln where it is heated up to very high temperatures that toughen it up. This way, properties like the water carrying capacity of the clay project are improved. The addition of glazing material to the body of the clay is another crucial procedure that must be done before the firing of the clay.

The process of glazing a clay project is to alter a couple of chemical properties that it possesses. It also allows it to be able to hold more water in it. At this stage, the clay project is referred to as being vitreous.

Understanding Handbuilding Pottery

Pottery is a craft that can either be done by hands or with the aid of a throwing wheel. When it is done with your hands, the craft is referred to as hand building. You get to create actual crafts with a clay lump in your hand and some other basic tools. You just need to know the basic techniques, and then you are good to go.

In the world of hand-building of pots, the three techniques that are mostly used involve the pinch pot technique, coil technique, and slab techniques. It is also very important that you get a mold of clay that you can easily work with. The best kind of clay to use should be something that has little or no resistance to pressure when impressed upon with your hands.

Lastly, when hand building your projects, you would be working majorly with your fingers, palms, and other very simple tools like a paddle and a rolling pin. With all of these, you get to create very beautiful projects. You also will be allowed the grace of expressing your creativity uniquely.

History of Pottery Making

The art of pottery-making dates as far back as the time when the early men roamed the earth. And the reason for that is because of the free availability of clay on the earth's surface. Fire was also discovered in the time of the early men. Once the clay works were fired, it was observed that they instantly became stronger and could be used for several other things.

The first kind of pottery projects to have been made at that time happened to be pinch pots. Pinch pots were made from round lumps of clay from which holes were made at the center by applying pressure. From there, the walls that rounded the holes are then raised and pulled up to whatever length.

The next pots formed at that time were the coil pots, which were made by building clay coils around a slightly thick base. The inner and outer edges were blended to achieve smooth and regular surfaces as the coils were built.

The coil pots and the pinch pots after they were made were usually heated or, better still, fired at low temperatures. This contributed to the fragility and reduced water holding capacity. When poured into them, water practically seeped right out, making them very unsuitable for any serious usage.

In a bid to solve the issue of fragility, the early potters usually added chunks of rocks or wood fibers to the body of the pots. That technique enabled them to get heated for longer hours, and consequently, higher temperatures. In the end, the pots got better but then ended up with black bodies due to the high flames.

To solve the issue of the black bodies, the early potters decided to fuse embellishing techniques by using tools to carve outlines on the bodies of the project while they were still soft enough. So, the clay projects were used to make all sorts of projects and were also used to represent the gods that made the people fertile.

Ancient Egypt and the Middle East at that period made use of clay when constructing their houses. This period fell in the range of 5000B.C and 4000B.C. The Egyptians especially had a lot more involvement with clay, and they were able to get them to do several useful things since they had kilns. The kilns were different in that the fire wasn't in contact with the pots. The fire usually was generated at lower chambers in the kiln. Then, the fire's heat was enveloped within the kiln, leading to the hardening of the clay projects. So, the issue of black pots was also settled here.

However, the early men from China still made their pots black, but then more embellished by using very exquisite glazing materials. They also designed the pots to have round bases, which were also stable. The Chinese also discovered the electric potter's wheel in 1000B.C. So, generally, they contributed a lot to the art of pottery making and the discovery of many useful glazes.

The other people who employed clay molding in their daily activities include the men from Columbia, Rome, and Liberia. The Romans in the early days directed their focus to the decoration of the pots. They were able to develop several ornate designs and techniques that made the art of pottery more beautiful. The early potters from Japan also contributed to pottery making but utilized their projects for religious purposes.

In the middle of the eighteenth century, pottery making became something that was traded. The potters in Europe sold out their clay projects at the markets or through interested merchants. However, the British potters contributed by working with glazing materials and by crafting the bodies of the clay projects in different designs. It was after the British potters started that others joined in working with their designs.

Composition of Pottery

Pottery, like was explained earlier, is a project made out of clay. But then, asides from clay, several other materials are involved in its production. Here, we will look at a few of them. Clay, which is the most elemental material, is made up of about 40% Aluminum oxide and about 46% Silicon oxide, with the rest being water.

Clay exists in two types, and they include the secondary and the primary. The primary clay is also known as the clay that is gotten right after a rock decomposes within the earth's crust. This kind of clay has not been moved to the upper surface of the soil by water or any other media, so it is free from sedimentary particles. The primary kind of clay is usually free from unwanted materials, heavy and thick.

The other kind of clay known as sedimentary clay is the clay that has been transferred to the upper surface of the soil through water and glaciers. It has a finer texture than the primary clay and comes out even lighter and less dense. Once the useful additives are fused with the primary clay, they can then be used for several purposes.

Clay could either be purchased or obtained in the form of a powder. So, to get it in a workable form, you'd have to add water to it and then have it mixed. It could also be obtained in moist and heavy masses. As for the big factories that work with clay, they obtain several mounds of clay and then refine them for use every day.

Another raw material need is the glazing material. The material is very useful when aiming to achieve uniformity or consistency in your clay projects. A high degree of similarity between your projects will be highly useful in cases where they are being sold in market environments. So, for that purpose, several glazes have been produced to fetch consistent results.

Glazing materials are made of different materials that merge as your clay project is being fired in the kiln. This fusion of the outermost glazing materials creates a layer that is resistant to water, and so, the clay container or vessel has an increased water holding capacity. For example, a vitreous is a pot with an absorption rate of less than 0.5%.

The components of glazing materials include sand and another component that makes the vessel vitreous. The vitreous-forming materials are those that make a clay project have the outlook of glass. They are found in the ground and also are made of flint and quartz. The two latter materials help to fasten the glaze to the body of the clay vessel. Then, it is also made of a refractory material that helps to solidify the glaze. Once the glaze is solidified, it'd also become stable.

The color of the glazing material is usually gotten from the oxides of metals. Antimony (a chemical element) will create a yellow color: copper; green, or turquoise blue, that of cobalt; black, that of chromium; green, and that of iron Nickel. There are other metallic oxides useful for coloring the glazing material, though.

The glazing material is usually bought in its dry forms. After, their weights are measured and then placed in ball mills. Water is then added to aid the mills in mixing the glaze into a paste-like substance. The mills also work to grind the glazing materials into the size of particles.

Health Benefits of Pottery

Pottery is an art that has a positive impact on your health and body in general. It provides some form of mental healing and helps those that practice them to relax. The beautiful thing about this art is that getting to work one's fingers through sand can go a long way to set one's mind, soul, and body as one. Here, we will discuss a few of the other benefits of pottery making.

1. Pottery allows you to express your creativity fully: Creativity is a pointer to uniqueness. And also, creativity can be birthed through series of crafting. Several pottery crafts out there mean just more than the clay from which they were molded. They represent actual emotions and feelings and end up giving the work an added twist. You could also get the chance to mold out something that anyone has never thought of before, especially if you will be selling your craft.

2. Pottery feeds your mind with an improved sense of optimism: Optimism is more like a heightened feeling of sureness of future situations. So, when you are down or feeling very sad, the art of crafting can help drive your mind away from the situation at hand. Then, you can get lost in a world where all you do is mold and create new designs.

3. It makes your sense of attention better: This benefit is for you if you either have a low attention span or find it hard to focus on anything at all. So, while molding your projects, you get to throw other matters off your mind and then focus intently on what is before you, which is your craft. This benefit doesn't just help you when you craft pots with clay. It could also come out to be very instrumental in other areas of your life.

4. It gives you the chance to search for new ideas and try them out: This benefit still boils down to creativity. If you have many ideas in your head, you could just draw out a template and then practice with a mound of clay. This benefit will also go a long way in seeing that you can understand your environment better than ever before.

5. It helps alleviate fatigue: Pottery is a craft you do with enthusiasm and the desire to try out your

creativity. And really, anything you do with such exuberance ends up leaving you more active and energized than ever before.

6. It helps you to flex the muscles of your hands, wrists, and arms: Pottery involves molding out curves and bends just to define your craft better. And for those techniques, you'd be working majorly with your fingers. Getting to move your fingers in such a fluid manner helps improve your dexterity and strengthen your joints.

7. Pottery crafting helps you to be more social than before: This benefit plays out best when you find a group of people who also like to work with mounds of clay like you do. That way, you get to exchange your ideas and then work on getting better together. From here, you would even discover that you find it much easier to start conversations when you are around people.

8. Pottery can help you to deal with pain: Pain can be birthed from stressful situations. But then, pottery has been proven to get rid of both stress and pain. Also, it helps your joints and muscles relax as you work through the clay.

9. It is a medium through which memories are captured: The existence of pottery was gotten from artifacts and other historical pieces of evidence. It was through this way that the art was preserved and transcended from one era to the other. So, by creating pottery projects, you are contributing something of importance to your era that can many years be referenced.

10. With pottery, you have the promise of a better life: Crafting allows you the freedom to express your emotions and skills. You get to push your mind to connect more dots and achieve bigger things. This way, you get to create new things and even make money out of them. And really, money does polish a person's life, as you can get for yourself anything that you want.

Chapter 2

Glossary of Pottery Making Terms

You need to be familiar with several terms as you progress with the craft of pottery making. And here, we will be looking at a few of them so that you can become conversant with them.

1. Absorbency: This term defines the extent to which a material can hold water within its pores. Every material has pores, so it is possible to either hold the water within it or let it go right through when you pour water within it. This term can also be referred to as the water holding capacity of a clay project. In the art of pottery, this term plays out in applying glazing materials to the body of projects.

2. Bisque: This term can also mean other words like bisque ware. A bisque can be defined as an already fired pottery piece. The process of firing usually helps in achieving a project with improved chemical and physical properties.

3. Black core: The black core is a term that is used to describe a clay body from which carbon hasn't been

driven out completely. Clay is a mass that contains some amount of carbon. So, when the body is fired in a kiln, the carbon gets oxidized to carbon (IV) oxide, which then leaves the clay body. In a situation in which the carbon is not completely oxidized, it remains trapped within the confines of the clay. The trapped gas then leads to the project becoming weak. A black core is usually formed during the process of firing a clay body via a reduction process.

4. Black hard: This term describes a stage during the drying of a clay project in which the clay cannot be easily beaten into different shapes. But then, even though it is not workable, it is not so dry that it is leather hard. And because the clay bodies still contain a little bit of moisture, they'd still have dark hues attached to them.

5. Bone China: This term is used to describe a clay body crafted in Britain during the eighteenth century to create an exact copy of the Oriental Porcelain. The directives used in the preparation of the Oriental Porcelain were kept covert. For the bone china, the clay body was only receptive to the slip-cast technique. Today, it is used in the production of dinnerware.

6. Burnishing: This is a process by which a black hard clay project has its body polished with a stone or glass shard. This way, your project comes out having a polished outlook. Pots made with this technique are usually not glazed, but fine slips are usually added to them. This process will help to improve the water holding capacity of a clay project.

7. Casting slip: This slip has a creamy consistency and is used in the production of ceramics. To work with a casting slip, pour the slip into a lubricated mold. After pouring in the slip, moisture is then extracted from the slip. The extraction then causes a thin layer of clay to be formed around the structure. Once the slip achieves the right density, it is taken out of the mold. After that, techniques like cleaning, glazing, and firing are carried out.

8. Ceramic change: This term describes a change that occurs when a clay body is heated to a temperature equal to or higher than a thousand Fahrenheit. At that temperature, the water molecules that are bound to the clay become free. Pottery that is fired at low heat cannot stand the test of time like the ones fired at the high-heat can.

9. Ceramics: This term is extracted from the Greek word; Keramos. The term means the clay of a potter. Ceramics are products that are made out of clay. It is also a term that describes the subject that a ceramicist studies. Ceramics has several uses in fields such as the production of medical supplies.

10. Cheese hard: This term is used to describe the first stage in drying a pottery craft that is still heavy with moisture.

11. China: This term is used by the English in the description of the imported ceramics from China. It also could mean a white clay body that has its body coated with a glazing material that can only be fired at low heat.

12. Clay: This term refers to an inorganic mound that is found to occur freely in nature. When water is added, it forms a thick paste that can be worked into different shapes and structures.

13. Clay body: A clay body can be defined as a mixture of clay and a few other essential minerals that affect the properties of clay. Another component of the clay body is the grog which makes it easier to work with clay. It also helps your projects to stand the test of time.

Whatever components of the clay body usually depend on the final project. Clay bodies are utilized in the production of porcelain and stoneware.

14. Coiling: This term is used to refer to the process of making worm-like clay piles. These worm-like structures are made of rolling clay with the inner surface of the palm. These coils are then used in building clay pots. But then, the lines or joints are usually not seen because they are blended as one.

15. Cones: Cones are small and have long bodies that are structured to meet at a particular temperature similar to the one good for the glazing material used. They can only be used once and can melt at different temperatures. Generally, cones are there to tell you the degree of melting observed in a kiln. Examples of these cones include Cone 1 and Cone 6.

16. Contraction: This term refers to a reduction in the size of a clay project due to a temperature change. This process is reversible, though. This term is useful because the rate at which glaze contracts must be the same as the rate at which the clay body contracts.

17. Crazing: This term has to do with an issue that is caused by different shrinkage rates of clay and the glazing material. It shouldn't be applied for pieces meant to be used as kitchenware.

18. Decorative: This term is used to describe a piece of ceramic that is only useful as an embellishment. Some of these decorative ceramic pieces include sculptures.

19. Dunting: This term refers to a process by which a clay project cracks due to its consequent firing and cooling. While it is being fired, the clay project undergoes a change that causes damaging stress to its walls. Dunting can also occur when the clay body and the glazing material contract or expand differently. It is also usually seen about a month after the clay project has been withdrawn from the kiln.

20. Earthenware: This is a term that encapsulates the clay projects that are fired at low temperatures.

21. Firing: This is the process of increasing the lifetime of a project by subjecting it to either low heat or high heat. Through this process, the clay particles and the glazing material are made to stand together as a more solid piece.

22. Flame ware: This refers to the awareness that can withstand the high degrees of heat when it is directly touching the tongues of a burning flame.

23. Food safety: This term specifies clay projects that are glazed with materials that are not harmful to a person's health. Glazing materials made out of lead or some other metal in the transition series could pose a lot of risk to a person's health.

24. Form follows function: This term chooses the design technique to implement for a particular project. The term also stresses the importance of uniformity between the form a clay project is in and the function it is meant to play out.

25. Frit: This term refers to the glazing materials mixed by melting them and then grinding them back into a powdery form. The resulting powder is then used to make other formulations of glaze.

26. Functional: This term refers to a piece of clay project in the category of ceramics that is not all that ornate. They usually have one purpose that they serve. So, they can be said to be the opposite of decorative pieces.

27. Glaze: This term describes a compound of coloring agents and materials that are ground into a powdery mix. When water is added to the powder, a sticky substance is formed, which is then applied to the surface of the clay project. When the glaze is heated, it melts and becomes glass-like.

28. Glaze fit: This term describes the extent to which the glazing material used for a project is compatible with the clay body used. The fit should be within a close bracket, though, to avoid issues such as crack lines.

29. Greenware: A stage that occurs before a clay project is fired in the kiln. This is also where several decorations are implemented on the body of the clay projects.

30. Grog: A substance with the same consistency as sand and is usually joined to a clay body to make it easy for you to work through it. Grog is more like clay that is fired at high heat and then ground into a granular form. It increases the resistance of clay bodies to thermal shock and cancels out the issue of shrinkage.

31. Hand building: This term refers to creating projects with the use of your fingers, palm, and a few other simple tools. The crafts made here are usually more decorative pieces.

32. High-temperature glaze: This refers to glazing materials that can withstand temperatures as high as 2200 Fahrenheit. They usually can stand the test of time and are of dull colors.

33. Intermediate glaze: These are glazing materials that can withstand temperatures within the range of 1900F and 2200F.

34. Kiln: A kiln is an oven-like structure that is used in firing clay bodies.

35. Lead: Lead is a principal element of glazing materials. The importance of this element comes out in the area of cooking ware. Lead is very harmful and should not be ingested in the body.

36. Leather hard: A point during the drying of a clay project that is completely free of moisture and cannot easily alter its shape.

37. Low-temperature glaze: Glazing materials that can withstand temperatures such as 1900 Fahrenheit.

38. Luster: This describes a metal additive that is found in glazing materials. They are usually soluble in some acids and are usually suspended in oil bases. Luster is

usually added to surfaces with the aid of brushes and can only withstand low temperatures.

39. Maiolica: This term describes a transparent clay project that can only withstand low temperatures. It is also coated with lead.

40. Majolica: It is a clay project with a clay body that is a pale yellow color.

41. Ovenware: This term refers to a craft that can withstand very high temperatures and mostly, is used in the kitchen.

42. Oxidation: This term refers to a process whereby oxygen is made to flow into the kiln to go into a reaction with certain elements in clay and the glazing material. This way, the naturally occurring carbon and sulfur in the clay are eradicated. The process takes place when the temperature in the kiln is in the range of 1300 and 2100 Fahrenheit.

43. Pinching: This refers to the process of crafting pots without using coils, slabs, or throw wheels. All you do is get a lump of clay and then press a thumb at the center to create a depression from which you work.

44. Porcelain: This refers to a clay craft that can withstand very high temperatures and is usually of very high quality. Porcelain can also stand the test of time and is also very strong.

45. Porosity: This term explains the process through which water molecules move up a clay lump via the action of capillarity.

46. Potter's wheel: This is a device with an upper disk that rolls about a clay lump. It gives a potter the grace to work several patterns on his clay projects, especially the clay cylinders.

47. Raku: This term refers to a group of ceramics that can only withstand low heat. These vessels usually do not serve a lot of purposes.

48. Reduction: This is a process in the firing of a glazed pot in which the oxygen attached to the metallic oxides in a clay or glaze mix is gotten rid of.

49. Salt glaze: This term refers to a glazing base to which the common table salt has been added. The process of salting a glazing material fetches a glaze that can stand the test of time.

50. Shrinkage: This term refers to a permanent reduction in the size of a piece of ceramic that occurs when it is dried and fired.

51. Slab: This is a structure that serves as the base for several clay projects. They are formed from mounds of clay that are pressed down and then cut out into different shapes.

52. Slip: This refers to a mix of clay, colorants, and water and is used on greenware to help it get dried easily.

53. Stain: This is a compound that adds color to glazing materials.

54. Stoneware: This is a toughened ware with a vitreous layer fired at temperatures higher than 2200F. In stoneware, the changes in the clay body and the glazing material are affected at the same rate. Stoneware is also wares that have gone through to the highest degree of hardening.

55. Temperature: This factor affects the extent to which clay bodies and glazing materials are fired. It is responsible for several factors like the durability and color of the glazing materials.

56. Throwing: This term describes a process involving pottery production by working with an electric throwing wheel.

57. Vitrification: This process is spurred by high temperatures. Once the clay mound is subjected to high heat, it first melts, after which it is left to cool. After cooling, the project assumes a glassy exterior. This process occurs when ceramics are fired, as some soluble components are converted to insoluble components.

58. Ware: This is a term that refers to all the pieces made out of clay. It is classified into ovenware, kitchenware, and several others that describe the functionality of the ware.

59. Wedging: This is a process by which unrefined clay is prepared into something that can be easily worked through. It helps to get rid of air spaces within the clay lump and also helps to ease the process of throwing clay lumps.

60. White hard: This is a term that is used to describe a stage in which a clay piece is devoid of moisture. This can be gotten within the confines of a preheated kiln.

Chapter 3

Pottery Making Tips and Tricks

Pottery tips and tricks will go a long way to help you craft the best pots. Here, we will be looking at a few of them and then discuss how you can implement them in your pottery-making craft.

1. Always engage yourself actively by practicing: When you practice. You end up becoming just good at crafting. So, apart from taking classes, you might need to slot out time to work independently and try out several techniques. This is where online lessons and e-books come to play. Practise will also allow you the grace to work on your skills generally.

2. Begin on a small scale at home: Once you are sure of your skills, you can start apportioning a room solely for your craft. Once you have many projects done, the room can become a temporary studio for you. Seeing your projects will encourage you to craft more and do better than you have done previously. What you mostly need for a studio at home include a table that can be folded

up and the other basic pottery tools. If you are the kind that prefers to throw clay lumps, you could get a small and cheap one. You might also want to get a shelf where you would store or display your projects.

3. Be comfortable with making first-time messes: The messiness of pottery making is actually what holds all of the fun. There will be several scenarios where clay would project towards walls and other surfaces. That is why you should always work with an overall that is impermeable to water if you do not plan on soiling your actual clothes. You should also ensure that you work in places where you can easily get of any mess made.

4. Start with loads of optimism: Most people would believe that they'd get the perfect projects the first minute they try. However, ninety percent of the time, it is hardly ever like that. That is why you would need a truckload of optimism and determination. If you do not get something right, do not stop. But then, continue at it until you get it done and done right.

5. When working with your clay, employ several strategies: You do not need a throwing wheel to make exquisite ware pieces. You could decide to work with your fingers and palm and still create the best pieces. Some other techniques that are receptive to the hand-

working idea include the formation of coils and slabs. With hand-building, you end up coming out with fantastic projects like bowls and even plates.

6. Merge yourself with a group formed by other potters: The good thing about these groups is that they have common facilities for their craftwork. So, you don't have to spend money purchasing kilns or glazing materials. You also get to relate with other creative people and then exchange meaningful ideas. For some of these groups, you might be required to pay a fee. But then, for some others, you don't have to.

7. Ensure that you enjoy yourself while crafting: The point here is being intentional about the pottery-making craft. You might also need to consider this tip if you plan on making the art of pot crafting a hobby.

Chapter 4

Pottery Making Process

When making pottery projects, several processes and guidelines are involved. So, here, we will be looking at these processes and studying what each entails.

Clay Preparation

The principal material needed for the production of pottery is clay. And here, the kind of clay being mentioned is the clay body. It has to be something that can be worked upon—soft and free of grit. A few potters used to get their clay by digging up the ground. Remember, clay is obtained from the decomposition of rocks within the earth's crust. So, they dig up the earth to find this primary clay.

However, the digging-up process can be time-consuming, and today, many potters have found it hard to continue with it. Apart from the issue of time to dig up the clay, the process also requires a lot of labor. So, the alternative is to buy the clay bodies they need from those that supply clay commercially.

Mostly, the best clay to use for your projects is the dark-colored clay bodies that have equal amounts of grog and sand. The two usually would help your project achieve a greater texture. Now, in refining clay from what is found in the earth to something usable for pottery, several processes must be followed through.

Wedging

This involves turning a body or lump of clay with your hand (majorly your fingers). The turning process requires placing the lump on a smooth or regular table, rolling it around, and then press firmly from above. The reason for this is to ensure that all the air spaces within the clay lump are eradicated. It also helps to ensure that the clay body is in one form.

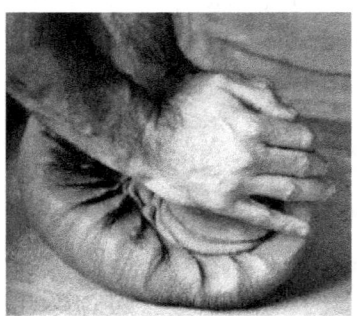

These air spaces or bubbles should be eradicated because of the process involved in the kiln. When you place a body of clay in the kiln, the air spaces could cause mini-explosions as they get bigger, and then, from there, they burst out. Once that happens, your project either crumbles or gets ruined. To know if there are bubbles of air within a clay lump, check the body for the presence of holes.

Forming

This is the next step after you have had your clay wedged.

It involves the techniques that you employ as you begin to work on your clay. And these techniques include the following;

- Slab
- Wheel
- Coil
- Pinch
- Mold

Drying

Once you rip through a clay bag, it begins to dry. The process of drying means that it gradually loses moisture and then gets hard. As it gets hard, the whole lump begins to shrink until it becomes very small. To prevent this process from occurring untimely, ensure that you wrap your clay projects with plastic coverings without holes to ensure that the moisture in them is preserved. Once that is done, you can then proceed to place the clay projects within shelves in some room with proper moisture in the air.

P.S: The plastic sheath or covering does not stop the loss of moisture, though. It only works to reduce it so that your clay body is soft enough to be worked with even days after you have prepared it.

However, as you sheath the clay body, you must carefully wrap the plastic around it. Pressing it too tightly can cause the shape to get disfigured. The pressure could also ruin your project since it will still be soft enough to be tampered with.

Leather Hard

After drying your clay body or project for a couple of days or more, it'd get to a point where it has the hardness of leather. Here, the clay body still has a relative amount of moisture, so it's only halfway dry. At this point, your project can still be tampered with.

What happens here is that moisture is lost from the body via a process of evaporation, and it causes the body to stiffen and then lose its elasticity. But then, the good side to this is that you get to run a carving knife across the body of your project to carve out the bits that are not too useful.

At this time, your project would have gained enough strength to support other structures like the handles, if there has to be, or some other ornate elements. So, generally, you get to alter the shape or figure of your project. The moment the little moisture in it here vanishes, you might not be able to do any more work on it.

Greenware

This stage is where your clay body or project has become white hard, i.e., a stage where it has completely lost all the moisture that it formerly contained via the process of evaporation. So, now, it can neither be bent or shaped. Any pressure or work done at this time will either lead to your project getting cracked into two or destroyed.

This is the stage where you should prepare your clay project to be fired in a kiln. So, the first thing you need to do is take the project away from the shelf of the room it was placed and then place it on the shelf of a less moisturized room. A kiln cannot be used for just a project, as it consumes a lot of energy and resources. So, you should store the clay project on the shelf until you have many other ones to stack in the kiln with it.

Bisque Firing

Once you get enough clay projects that you can dry up in the kiln, you can proceed to get them fired. There are two stages involved in this process, and the first stage occurs at a temperature of about 180-degree Fahrenheit. Once your project is passed through the kiln at this temperature, it gets hard enough to be handled without the risk of having it broken when it is being glazed. The porosity of the clay at this level is still retained, though. Porosity has to do with the water-holding capacity of the project.

So, when you apply the glazing material to the walls of the clay project, the part of it that the clay can absorb is absorbed. Once the moisture is absorbed, the glaze then remains on the surface of the bisque ware. The bisque firing procedure goes on for about three days, and on the first day, all you need to do is load your clay projects into the kiln and then set it on.

From there, reduce the heat so that your projects dry. Then, you can leave them there throughout the night to become just warm to be handled. If you fired the clay project too quickly, you could end up having a destroyed work.

On the second day, you can increase the temperature of the kiln until you achieve a temperature of about 1800-degree Fahrenheit. Once that is achieved, you can go on to turn off the kiln. However, you should not immediately proceed to get your projects out. You would still need their temperature to get cooled down.

Once the temperature in the kiln drops, your project is now referred to as bisque ware.

Glazing

This is the process that involves the production of the glazing material. The glazing material is made of the powdery form of glass, clay, colorants, and water. The glazing material is applied to the surface of the clay using any of the following processes;

- Dipping
- Pouring
- Spraying
- Brushing
- Sponging

In some cases, two or more of the techniques above are usually used together. Ensure that the foot ring of your project is free from the glazing material and that the pot is made from a stoneware clay body. When you are done, you can then move your pottery to a glaze shelf. The glazed projects are stored on this shelf until they are many enough to be loaded in a kiln.

Glaze Firing

This is a process that goes on for about three days at a temperature of about 2350-degree Fahrenheit. Several types of kilns can be used for glaze firing per the fuel used, such as wood, oil, gas, and electrically powered kiln.

Once the pots have stayed in for that long, you can then proceed to get them out of the kiln and store them on some other shelf.

Overglaze Firing

This procedure is carried out in a case where you want to have your project painted to a particular color or designed with a particular pattern. Some of these ornate patterns include the application of luster, decals, and china paints.

So, once you place them back in the kiln, they get fired at a temperature of about 1300-degree Fahrenheit. The temperature ensures that the colors come out brighter and more lustrous. You could also increase the temperature to about 2350-degree Fahrenheit to achieve the best results.

The only issue with the over-glaze firing procedure is that the over-glaze is not permanent. It could easily be removed when a surface is run against it. So, eventually, the over-glaze is removed. However, because of this issue, techniques like the painting of

China have been adapted, and they include applying several layers of over-glaze to the fired works. The several layers at the end of the day contribute to the very splendid designs.

A Short message from the Author:

Hey, I hope you are enjoying the book? I would love to hear your thoughts!

Many readers do not know how hard reviews are to come by and how much they help an author.

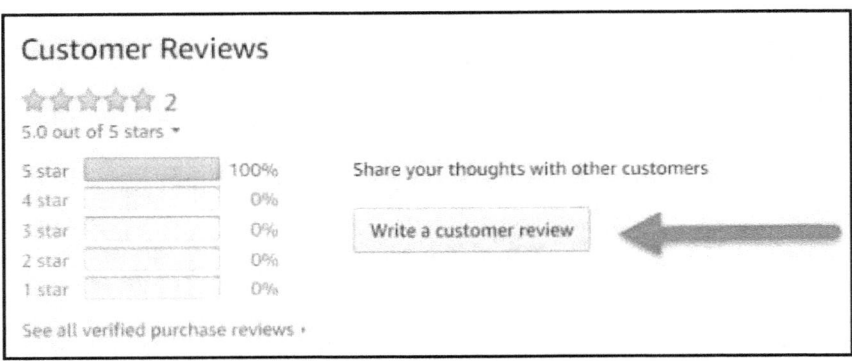

I would be incredibly grateful if you could take just 60 seconds to write a short review on Amazon, even if it is a few sentences.

\>> Click here to leave a quick review

Thanks for the time taken to share your thoughts!

Chapter 5

Getting Started With Pottery Making

As a beginner with little or no idea about making pottery projects, we will look at a couple of important sections to help you craft your first pottery project.

Basic Tools, Supplies, and Equipment

There are a couple of tools, supplies, and equipment you would be working with as you make pottery crafts, so ensure you properly familiarize yourself with them.

Tools

Most of the tools you'd be working with as you proceed as a beginner include the ones you would need to construct a clay body with your hand or throw clay lumps on a potter's wheel. But then, note that not all the tools mentioned here are totally necessary for the art of pottery. They are mostly included here as they help to make your project easier and more refined.

Wedging Board/ Workbench

A wedging board is a surface where you wedge your clay before undergoing further work on it. They are usually large wooden boards with regular surfaces where you can work your clay upon. The process of wedging clay lumps has already been discussed above.

Before you choose any wedging board, several factors must first be considered, and here, we will discuss a few. First, you could choose to make the board yourself. And really, it does not involve any stressful technique as all you need to do is get a platform with a regular surface. The board could be made from plaster. The consequence of plaster being at the surface of your wedging board is for you to be able to reclaim your clay easily. The plaster helps to draw water out of the clay body, and that inevitably gets it to grow a bit harder. So, to make the plaster coat absorb less moisture, you could make the surface wet before you begin to wedge your clay on it.

It could also be a plasterboard coated with canvas or a plywood board coated with canvas.

You could also choose to work with surfaces made out of granite, concrete, or Masonite. If you don't like the idea of constructing a board yourself, you could choose to buy one online.

If you are going to be using the board in a studio, it is advised that you go for the ones you can easily move around the studio. You should also consider how easily you can store the boards after you have used them. But then, if you know that you would be doing more of clay wedging, you might want to get aboard with legs—like in the form of a table.

Aprons and Towels

The art of pottery requires that you work with clay, and clay, when moist, can be very messy. So, to avoid a scenario where your clothes get soiled up and messy, too, it is advised that you tie an apron around your neck. You could also see that you have a towel beside you that can absorb water to a large extent. You could get a small towel to clean your hands intermittently as you work and a much larger one to spread across your laps when throwing your clay on a throwing wheel.

Chamois

This piece of leather is used in pressing against the outermost edges of thrown ware. It could also be very useful when you need to make the surface of a piece of leather-hard smooth and regular. But then, before you use it, ensure that you sprinkle a bit of water across the surface and that you wash it immediately after use. That way, you wouldn't have a situation where the clay sticks to the surface stubbornly.

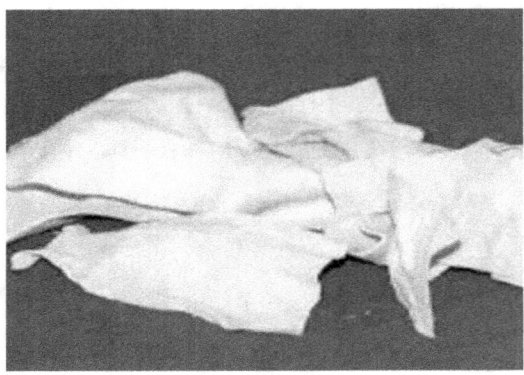

Potter's Needles

These needles are one of the commonest and most important tools used in the art of pottery making. They usually have handles made out of wood, metals, or plastic and are used to work on the uppermost edges of your projects while they are being thrown on the electric wheel. And if you are working with the hand-building procedure, you could use the needles to score your slabs and coils.

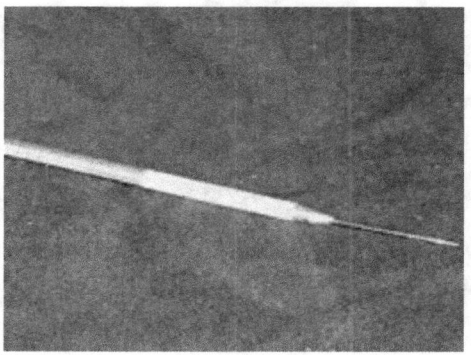

Cut-Off Wires

These wire strings have a look similar to that of a wire cheese cutting tool. Sometimes, fishing lines or springs that have been untwisted from their coils could be used as suitable replacements. These cut-off wires are useful when you need to break down large bits of clay into smaller lumps. It can also be very useful when you need to peel off the base of a thrown clay project from the surface of a throwing wheel. If you work with the replacement option, you have to ensure that they are flexible enough.

Fettling Knives

These are knives with thin blades. They have tempers that are either hard or soft. The hard ones are usually very rigid, while the soft ones come out with flexibility that can help them be turned through angles and curves.

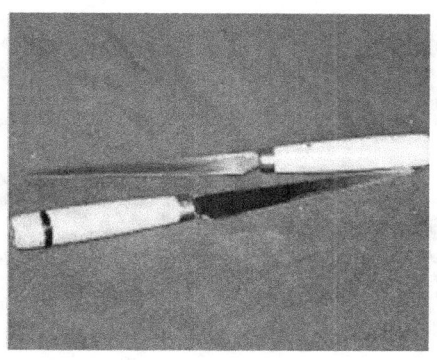

Most of these knives are used to get rid of fettles. Fettles are the lines that appear when you merge two pieces of mold. They are very useful when you need to have a square of slab trimmed across its length. If you have several types of fettling knives, it is advised that you have them marked so that you can easily separate one from the other.

Ribs and Scrapers

These two tools are very useful when throwing pots or other clay vessels on a wheel. They are used to maintain the shape of whatever structure it is that you are throwing on the wheel. They also help to ensure that your projects have a smooth and regular surface.

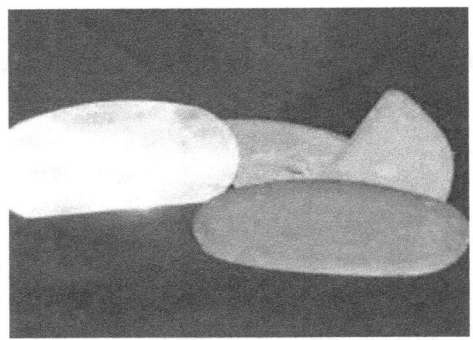

When building your pots with the 'coil' technique, you will definitely need the ribs as they would help blend one coil onto another. There are different kinds of ribs that you can use when making pottery, and indeed, they come in different sizes and shapes. They are built either out of wood or rubber.

Scrapers have a lot of resemblance to a rib, but then, it has a much lighter weight and is used to work on wet or leather hard clay projects. You'd find them in several shapes and sizes and are usually made out of either steel, rubber, or wood. When making pottery, you could work with both the rib and the scrapers— they help provide clean finishes.

Loop, Wire, and Ribbons

These tools are used together when you need to cut off the excess clay from your projects. You would also need them when you need to build up your projects with your hand. However, we wouldn't recommend that you work with them when throwing your pots on a wheel as they are too weak to withstand too much pressure.

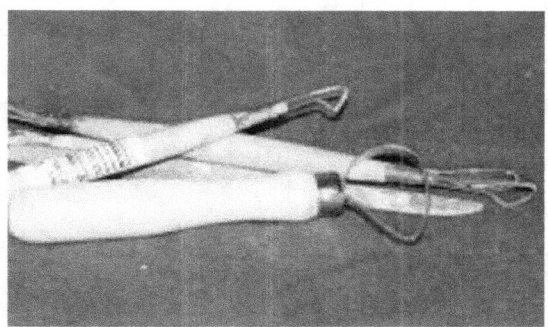

Wooden Modeling Tools

These tools are useful when building your pottery with your hand. They come in several shapes, but then, most have their heads shaped in triangles. So, if you ever need to trim your pottery while it is still rolling on the wheel, you could choose to work with it.

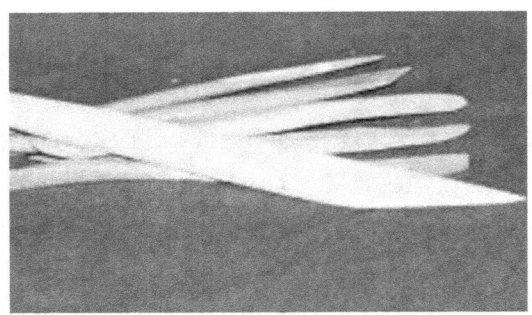

Sponges

This is necessary as you might be in a situation where your project gets too dry or too wet. Running a sponge around the walls will immediately help to solve the issue. There are different sponges, either small, medium, or large, and they are all useful in throwing pottery.

Potter's Calipers

They are used in taking measurements of the inner and outer diameters of the mouth of your project. For example, if you need to measure the diameter of the cover you need for a jar, a pair of calipers will go a long way to help. You could also use it to measure the base of whatever project you are working on—pitchers, saucers, etc. They are constructed out of either metal, wood, or plastic.

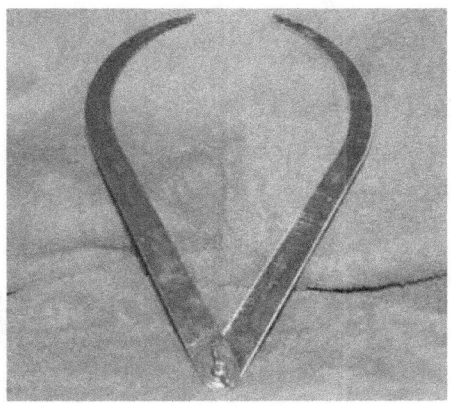

Rolling Pin

This tool is used when you need to roll out a lump of clay into a flat slab. For your pottery project, you could choose to work with any rolling pin you desire. But then, to be on the safer side, you could decide to work with the twelve-inch rolling pin or something larger, depending on the size of projects you work on. In the design utilized in some rolling pins, the pins roll separately from the handles, but then the whole body rolls in others.

Supplies and Equipment

Besides the tools mentioned above, you would also need a couple of supplies and equipment as listed below.

Pottery Clay

Clay is a naturally occurring inorganic material that is obtained from the decomposition of rocks within the earth's crust. It consists of fine grains that form a sticky puddle when wet. It also has other constituents like sand, mineral elements, and other natural elements of the soil, which occur in different quantities. Clay also occurs in several consistencies—i.e., texture and hues, and all of those qualities depend on the size of the individual particles.

Clay appears red or a rusty shade of brown when rich in Iron (III) oxide. The lumps of clay devoid of inorganic compounds usually appear gray or a very pale white. It's such pale varieties that are known as porcelain clay.

There are also three kinds of clay that are used in the art of pottery, and they include the following;

1. Stoneware
2. Earthenware
3. Porcelain clay

All of the clay types listed above have different functions that they serve and can also be fired at a specific temperature range. Another factor that differentiates them is the rate at which they absorb water or shrink.

The stoneware clay is the one that offers little to no resistance when it is worked upon. It is commonly used in several pottery projects out there and is the best option for beginners. The stoneware clay also comes in different colors, ranging from white to a dark shade of brown. When any project that is made out of the stoneware clay is taken through the firing process, it comes out having the non-porous characteristic. And that inevitably cancels the need to glaze the project.

Earthenware is denser than the stoneware clay, and even with a lot more weight, but then offers a smaller strength in comparison. It also doesn't offer too much resistance when it is being worked upon. But then, once it is fired, it comes out being porous. So, if your projects are not glazed at the end of the day, it ends up being unable to hold water in it. This kind of clay is not usually recommended for beginners because it requires that the final project be glazed.

The last clay type is porcelain clay. This one offers a whole lot of resistance and might not come out being too easy to mold. So, if you are going to work on it at all, you would need to add in a whole lot of water to get it in the right consistency. If it's not moist enough, it ends up getting dry. If it also comes out being too moist, it could also fall to its base quickly. So, if you are going to work with this kind of clay, you would need to put in lots of time to properly work with it and understand how to get it in the right consistency. So, this option is also not ideal for beginners.

Glaze and Other Decorating Materials

After making your pottery or other clay vessels, you could also embellish it with ornate designs. And even though there are several options to choose from, it is best for you as a beginner to work with glazing materials or any other paint base. You can then move on to working with more complicated procedures like carving out designs.

The glaze technique is one of the ideal techniques that a beginner can employ in pottery. The glaze has the consistency of fluid, and so, when applied on the walls of clay vessels, it works to give it a glassy outlook. Glazes also are available in several colors and can be used to make your projects waterproof.

However, when it comes to painting options that are best for beginners, you could work with the ones with latex bases. Acrylic paints are also wonderful choices you can work with for decorating your pottery. Overall, both the glazing materials and the paints are not too costly and can easily be found online or in any store where art supplies are sold.

Pottery Wheel

Pottery wheel helps you to make better pottery. It is more like an advanced choice for beginners, but then, even with that, you should invest in a pottery wheel as it will help you get better and get more rewarding results. Most of these wheels can either be powered manually or electrically, and each has its advantages and disadvantages.

The best choice for a beginner should be purchasing a small-sized electric throwing wheel. Wheels that are powered electrically usually do not require that you develop an arrangement that gets the wheel rolling to get the right shape. The other advantage an electric wheel will fetch you is the provision of more torque and a channel through which you can regulate the wheel's speed.

You also should watch out for the ease by which you can change the parts of the wheel when buying a throwing wheel. You do not want to get something that requires many complicated processes just to change one or two parts.

Manual throwing wheels have their speeds controlled by the speed at which the wheel is pedaled by the potter's foot. So, the potter gets the choice to slow down the speed to whatever rate that he desires.

Kiln

This is another essential piece of equipment that you would frequently be using as you work in the art of pottery making. This equipment is used to fire your clay projects. It is also used to ensure that the layers of glazes applied to the surface of a clay project stay in place. Kilns also work to make your clay project last longer.

The only reason why you wouldn't want to fire your clay project should be because it won't be coming in touch with water frequently. However, you should ensure that you have them fired in a kiln for tableware and other utensils.

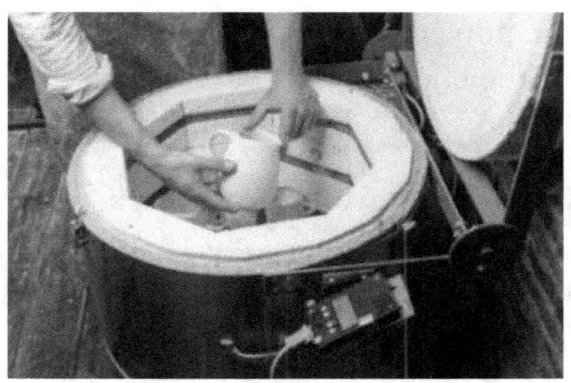

There are different kinds of kilns that you can work with, and they include those constructed out of heat-impermeable wooden planks, gas kilns, and electrically powered kilns. As a beginner, it is required that you work with those that are electrically powered, as you don't have to go through the hassle of setting anything up. Apart from that, you also get a guide that would help you make maximum use of your kiln and regulate the temperature easily.

The small kilns usually have plugs that you can plug into sockets buried into walls. Larger kilns may require more complex electrical fittings, making it less ideal for you as a beginner. It could also require that you spend much more to get it fitted up in place.

For beginners, the Skutt Kilns come out as a great option. They produce strong fires that are capable of stirring up a powerful rush of heat. The Skutt 714 brand is an excellent choice for a beginner as it has all the required features packed in one machine.

Setting Up Your Pottery Making Workspace

Getting your pottery studio in order is very essential in crafting pottery pieces. Clay pottery is very fragile and is very susceptible to breaking, so you want to ensure that the paths leading to your work shelves are cluster-free. Here, we will be discussing a couple of factors that will go a long way in helping you set up a workspace for your pottery crafts.

1. Getting your equipment ready: The kind of equipment that you use for your pottery craft determines how you will set up your workspace. One thing to be considered is the reason for being a potter. If you are making pottery crafts as a pastime, you may not need too many tools and equipment. And you may not use too much equipment to set up your workspace.

If you intend molding as a pastime, all you need is a throwing wheel, a work surface, and a rack for your pottery. If you are also a potter that works with the hand-building technique, you'd only be needing these; a slab rolling device, a working surface, and a small rack for storing your pottery.

The kind of equipment employed in the art of pottery differs from one person to the other. However, before you spend any money on pottery equipment, ensure that you know what it is that you need. You also need to know on what scale you would be molding the pottery. If you are molding commercially, you would need to get several pieces of equipment.

Pottery is a craft that involves several stages and procedures, so you want to ensure that the kind of tools you use to correspond with the level of activity in your studio. If you are engaging in pottery to craft out small pottery projects, you wouldn't need to purchase too much large equipment.

There are several kinds of equipment used in pottery, most of which have been discussed earlier. However, for this section, we will consider a couple of them briefly. That will go a long way in helping you know how to get things in order.

- Pottery wheel: This piece of equipment usually takes most of the space in a workstation. The size usually is determined by how it is powered—either manually or by an electrical force. A few other things should be considered before you get a pottery wheel, and they include the following;

- The size of the motor powering the wheel
- The reversibility of the wheel—whether it is controlled with the left hand, right hand, or both hands.
- The brand of the throwing wheel. The Brent branded wheels are known to stand the test of time. The Speedball brand is known to have produced tons of pottery wheels. The Nedic-

Shimpo brand can be worked within buildings because of how quiet it is.

- The slab roller: This equipment is something you should get if you plan to work with the hand-building technique. Some of the slab rollers being sold out these days can be mounted on tables, which helps save a lot of space in the room.

- Kilns: You can choose to work with different kinds of kilns when setting up your workstation. The kiln is mostly either powered by electricity or gas. There are also computerized and manual kilns. The beautiful thing about these kilns is that they all fit into whatever activity goes on in your workshop.

The kilns that are powered electrically are usually a lot cheaper than those powered by gas fuels. So, if you are looking for an economical option that you can work with without stress, you should opt for electrically powered kilns. Advanced potters usually handle the ones powered by gas fuels because the kilns can add more designs to the projects.

When comparing manual and computerized kilns, you would notice that the computerized ones are easier to manipulate and work with. On the other hand, the manual ones can stand the test of time while still offering the best results.

The difference that exists between a kiln that is loaded from the front and the one that is loaded from the back is majorly dependent on the price incurred in obtaining them. The ones you load from the front are usually easier to work with and will only pose issues when picking up pottery from the end of the kiln. The kilns you load from the top are good choices if you don't plan to work at a high-scale level.

- Worktable: The work table is one piece of equipment that should be found in the middle of your workstation. To get the best effect and results, you should ensure that it is neither too tall nor too short. The best height for your work table is something at the level of your hips.

You should also ensure that your work table has a spot on it where you can work upon mounds of clay. It should also have a spot for clay wedging. The surfaces on which the wedging is done mustn't be something that clay can stick to. Surfaces made out of oak, maple, or even plywood are good options.

However, if you will work with a canvas on your work table, you must ensure that it is firmly secured to the joints underneath the table. The surface of the canvas should also be without creases.

Your work table should also have a bottle of water with a perforated nozzle that allows you to moisten your projects and hands as you work. It can also go a long way in helping you beat down the dust particles suspended in the air around your workstation.

- The glaze table: This is the surface where you get your pottery glazed. This table must be placed at a very far point from the major table for molding your clay. This way, you wouldn't have to be bothered that the glazing material would ruin your pottery project.

However, if you are working in a studio so small that you cannot have a table for glazing operations, ensure that you clean up your workstation before and after running through the glazing techniques. You could also set a protective covering on the surface of your work table to keep things clean.

Whatever glazing table you choose to work with must have a working table wide enough to accommodate all your pottery for a particular project.

- Storage shelves: Shelves are needed majorly to differentiate between bisque ware and other glazed ware. If you are working on a small scale, you could get only one shelf for this purpose. But then, for large-scale pottery, you would need to get several shelves to prevent the projects from mixing up. This technique will also help to prevent tampering with your pottery projects.

Some potters also have shelves for storing their equipment, just to keep things orderly and neat. Most times, for those who work on a large scale, the equipment contributes to the activity within the workstation. Examples of this equipment include portable tools and other small equipment.

To save space in your workstation, you should ensure that you do not place the shelves at the same site in your studio. The more distance you place between the shelves, the less clustered your workstation will seem. You could also go for customized shelves when choosing your work shelves.

- A damp room: This room is a compartment that you store your unfinished potteries. The one factor you should consider when choosing a damp room is the humidity level in your workstation. This room prevents a scenario where your pottery completely loses its moisture before you finish work on it.

If you do not plan on spending too much money on this, you could opt for an old and dysfunctional refrigerator that is still well-shelved. Apart from acting as a damp room, it would also go a long way in ensuring that your ceramic pieces do not get destroyed. Another option is to use plastic sheaths to cover your pottery.

- A tool shelf: A rack with a cart above it can be best for storing your tools. The cart will stay well on the racks, and the cart can also be a good housing site for your tools. This way, you get to access the tools easily.

2. Storing your clay: Clay can contribute largely to the activity in your workstation. To control this, you should store the mounds in containers or tightly sealed plastic-sheathed bags. These bags, you could arrange beneath your work table, to keep things tidy. While storing your clay, you should also ensure that you keep a mop around to prevent mold growth.

3. Getting your tools: The tools that you need for your workstation include the following; ribs, scraping tools, potter's needle, cut-off wire tool, sponges, calipers, fettling knives, and other tools already discussed in the tools, supplies, and equipment section.

4. Planning out the space in your workstation: This is the next stage after you must have gotten all the necessary tools arranged in place within your workstation. Here is the section that places heavy

emphasis on mapping out areas for your pottery crafting and storage of your tools.

First of all, you could choose to have your workstation based in your house or outside your house, maybe in the garage. The amount of space you have to work with doesn't matter as long as you can keep everything in its right areas and squares.

One thing that goes a long way to reduce the activity in a workstation is using wheels. Having all your equipment and shelves on wheels will go a long way to ensure that you can create space as easily as possible without much physical effort. So, when you need space, you could just pull it towards the walls.

Now, we will look at a couple of other things to note when setting up your workstation.

> 1. Work with a floor that is constructed out of Vinyl or Linoleum. You should also ensure that you have a mop around to get rid of spillages easily.

> 2. Do not set carpets on your floors. When clay lumps land on carpets, they end up becoming dust particles. So, the best thing is to get a floor mat that you could use to get rid of dust.

3. Ensure that your workstation is well equipped with enough power outlets, especially if you would be working with electrical pottery appliances. You could also work with plug extensions in case there aren't many sockets.

4. Ensure that your workstation is equipped with as many water outlets as possible. You should also ensure that your workstation station is well equipped with buckets and other water containers. However, ensure that you get some other outlet for your glazing materials to prevent a situation where they get clogged.

5. Ensure that you place your turning wheels close to a socket. When your turning wheel is working, there could be many incidences of splashes, and those could do a lot to mess up your workstations. So, it is best to place your wheel at a place where you could deal with the messes.

6. You should devote a section of your workstation to all the things you have to do with clay. So, here, you just wedge your clay and do

other works on it. Most times, more than half of your workstation is dedicated to clay.

7. Keep your glazing compartment separate from the other compartments.

8. Map out a portion of your workstation where you can store your glazing materials in both powdery and liquid states.

9. Your kiln should be set in the same corner as the shelves upon which you arrange your pottery projects. The Kiln should also be in a place that is not prone to fire disasters.

10. Set your kiln in a place just by the door if you need to escape from a hazard.

11. Use your kiln in a room with cross ventilation. You should also ensure that your kiln's vents are directed outside.

Safety Guidelines For Pottery Making

Even though it comes out as being very interesting, the art of making pottery has a lot of hazards attached to it.

So, here, we will be looking at the various safety procedures you need to note.

1. Ensure that you do not leave your clay exposed: When clay sits for a while, especially if it hasn't yet been worked upon, the surface becomes a bit dusty. When in contact with air, that dust can choke it with impure inorganic substances known as silicate dust. So, to avoid this issue, ensure that you constantly moisten your clay projects to prevent the dust lying on its bodies from finding its way into the air. You could also ensure that you regularly have your clay projects trimmed.

2. Use moist towels and foams to wipe across your clay projects to capture silicate particles and dust that might have settled on your pottery. This procedure is very necessary, especially in a scenario where you have repeatedly had your clay trimmed or glazed. You should also ensure that you constantly wipe across the surface of your pottery projects.

3. Store powdery supplies in air-tight compartments: Doing this will ensure that the air remains free from dust particles and that it can stay down for a long period. Also, you need to note that powders can easily get turned into paste if water were to get into them, which could immediately make them very useless.

4. Set your kiln in the right location: The right place you should set your kiln in should be somewhere with a lot of ventilation. It should also be a very close place to the door so that in case there is a fire; you'd be able to escape immediately. You should also ensure that the kind of floor you set your kiln upon is not susceptible to melting. If you are even going to set your kiln close to shelves, ensure that they are metallic.

5. Set up emergency plugs for your electrically powered devices: For kilns and other devices that are powered by electricity, ensure that you have a switch that can immediately shut them down in case of any issue. The other devices that make use of electricity include drilling machines and turning wheels. It'd even be much better if all of these machines have their wiring connected to this one plug.

6. Ensure that you clean all the tools you use for molding your pottery after using them: To ensure that your tools do not deteriorate their quality as you use them, ensure that you clean them the moment you are done. This way, you can prevent issues like silicate build-up and rusty metallic surfaces.

7. If you have containers with dangerous and harmful contents, ensure that you keep them lidded. This

technique will help prevent spills and go a long way to protect you from burns. You should also ensure that the dangerous chemicals are kept in bottles that are properly tagged. If the chemicals are highly toxic, it is advised that you place warning signals to the bodies of the bottles containing them to keep yourself and others safe.

8. In case any of the processes in your pottery art releases very dangerous fumes, it is recommended that you have a vent that pumps it right out. Having to inhale these toxic fumes can be very bad, and you could even end up falling very sick as a result. If you cannot afford to have a vent fixed, you should get a ventilator.

9. Clean the studio as often as possible. Working with clay means that you also would be working with water. And definitely, you would at one moment or the other have something spilled to the floor. The best way to handle this mess is by cleaning the floor with a mop. You should also ensure that you wipe across surfaces to ensure that silicate hasn't settled about.

10. Have your studio properly ventilated: When you haven't had your studio cleaned up in a long time, you should fix a ventilating machine that would help you to

flush out the dust particles from wherever they are settled in the studio. You could do this by opening up the windows and doors that lead to the studio.

11. You can keep yourself safe by always ensuring that you fix a ventilator to your face: Ventilators are very important when dealing with activities that stir up a whole lot of dust. When those particles saturate the air, there's a high possibility of you breathing them in. And once that happens, it could cause damage to a person's lungs.

12. Ensure that you wear the right shoes, which should protect your toes. Having to let go of a tool suddenly or hotly glazed pottery can break the bones in your leg if you aren't too careful.

13. If you have injuries, tend to them. The kind of wounds that you could have when working with clay include burns and cuts. That is why it is more than necessary for you to have a first aid kit fixed somewhere in your workstation. Having your wounds tended will also go a long way to protect you from skin infections and other health issues.

14. Ensure that you wash your hands often: When you are done throwing clay or glazing your pottery, ensure

that you immediately wash your hands to prevent them from cracking. Not cleaning your hands could also mean that you get glaze into your nose, eyes, or mouth in case you touch your face.

15. Wear protective eye goggles: These goggles will go a long way to help when you trim your pottery. Sometimes, when grinding your clay lumps, a couple of the lumps could fly off at a tangent, and that could be harmful to your eyes if they aren't protected.

Pottery Forming Techniques

Different techniques can be utilized when making pottery, and here, we will discuss the various techniques. Most of them are very suitable for beginners and will work best for the hand-built pottery formation.

Slab Pots

Slab pottery is formed from slabs. Slabs are flattened piles of clay on which the walls for pots are built upon. If they aren't square, they'd be in the shape of a cylinder. When structuring a slab pot, the following procedures are usually carried out;

1. Roll out a lump of clay with a rolling pin.

2. Cut the slab into the desired dimensions with the use of a clay knife. You could ensure that the dimensions are uniform by working with a template.
3. Score the edges where the slabs meet, and then run a layer of slip across the scored edges.
4. Now, press the slipped edges firmly together to ensure cohesion.
5. Make a clay coil by rolling a soft clay mound across a smooth surface.
6. Fix the coil to the point where the slabs meet.
7. Blend the edges of the coil with the body of the slab until the lines vanish.
8. Build up the walls of the pottery by adding more coils.

Pinch Pots

A pinch pot is formed from a whole lump of clay, and usually, there are no joints or ridges that need to be blended into each other. It may look simpler to construct compared to slab pots, but there are a couple of techniques requiring many complex steps.

The size of the lump you work with when forming a pinch pot depends largely on the size of pottery that you want to build up. If you are going to make a small pot, you should work with a small lump of clay, and vice versa. Below are the guidelines for making a pinch pot.

1. Grip a lump of clay in your hand.
2. Press a thumb to the center of the clay.
3. To widen the hole formed by your thumb, exert more force at the center with your thumb. Once you go through with this procedure, you would get a small and thick pot.
4. You would then progressively work on the walls by pulling them up until they become thinner. To get this procedure done nicely, you would need to press against the interior and exterior walls pretty firmly. You could also add coils of clay to your project if you notice the walls getting thinner.
5. Once the walls are just at the right density, you can then go on to run a rib across the exterior surfaces to make them smooth and regular. You could also trim the edges of your pottery too.

Coil Pots

The coil pots are pots made from hand-built techniques. They can also produce all kinds of pots, no matter the design or the sculpture to be worked with. Now, we will look at the procedures that guide the formation of coil pots.

1. To get a slab that you can work with for your pottery, use a rolling pin to flatten a lump of clay. If you plan to make pottery with a round bottom, you should work the slab into a puki. And if you are working on making pottery with a flat base, you can work on a flat board.
2. Make a clay coil that is half an inch long in diameter.
3. Fix the coil all around the bottom of the pottery you are molding.
4. To continue building, add more coils of clay to the preexisting bases. As you build, though, ensure that you blend the ridges of one coil with the others. You could use your fingers or a wooden palette for this procedure.
5. When you are done, run the edge of a rib across the inner and outer surfaces to get them regular. This way, the ridges between the coils don't come out being too defined.
6. If your pottery isn't still at the right height, you can go on to merge more coils of clay into the existing ones.
7. When you are done, trim the edges with a wire string.

Wheel-Thrown Pottery

This pottery refers to the kind of pottery that is done on an electric wheel. The electric wheels are also known as the potter's wheels. They work by rotating clay bodies that are pressed to their surface around circles. This machine is best for those that want to produce several potteries in little time.

The procedures below describe how the wheel is used.

1. Place a lump of clay at the center of the wheel.
2. Power on the wheel, and then set it to your desired speed settings. The high speed sets the wheel moving very quickly, and the low-speed setting sets the wheel moving slowly. The intermediate of the two speeds is known as the medium speed setting.

3. Once the two steps above are done, you can continue with either of the techniques discussed above.

Slip Cast

This technique is another way of producing pottery on a large scale. It is also a way to make several pottery pieces that look very much like each other. This system is mostly used by those who make pottery to make a profit. The customers usually would demand that there is a regularity in the products supplied. And so, because of that, the potters work with molds. All that is done here is for the clay to be prepared. Usually, the clay is made with the consistency of a fluid. Once that fluid is poured into molds, the pottery is then formed.

Chapter 6

Pottery Making Project Ideas

Handbuilt Coil Pot

Tools and Supplies

- Lump of clay
- Clay knife
- Rolling pin or extruding tool
- Slab roller
- Rib
- Wooden paddle
- Plastic covering
- Moist foam

Procedures

1. Press down a clay lump by running a rolling pin repeatedly across the surface. You could also work with a slab roller to get the base flat and thin. Work towards achieving a thickness of about 1/4-inches.

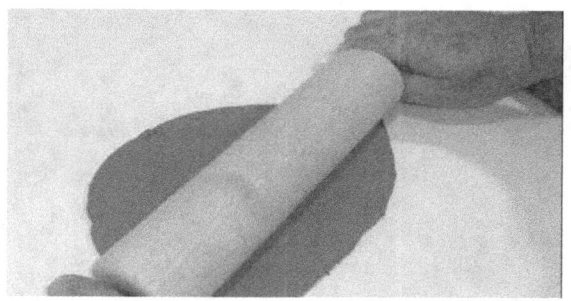

2. Cut out the flattened slab until you get the exact dimension that you need for your pot. Ensure that you trim the slab around the edges and not across the surface.

3. On another board, roll another lump of clay with your two hands. As it moves across the board, you should notice it getting longer and finer. You could also use an extruding device to get this done. However, ensure that you cover the coils with plastic wrap as soon as you are done to prevent them from drying out.

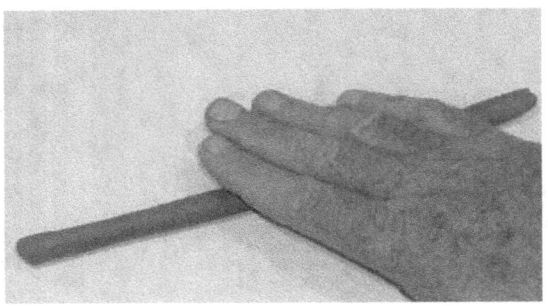

4. Now, you can gently lift the rolled-out coil and press it to the sides of the base you made in the first procedure. As you roll it in, ensure that your fingers press against the sides firmly to create a firm adhesion.

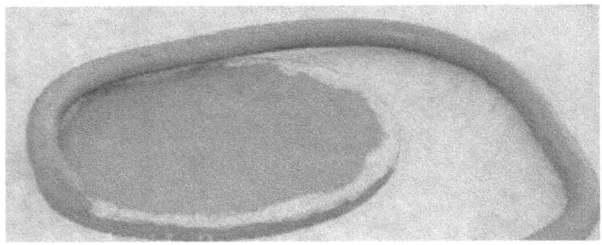

5. Trim off the length of the coil that remains after you have set it around the base.

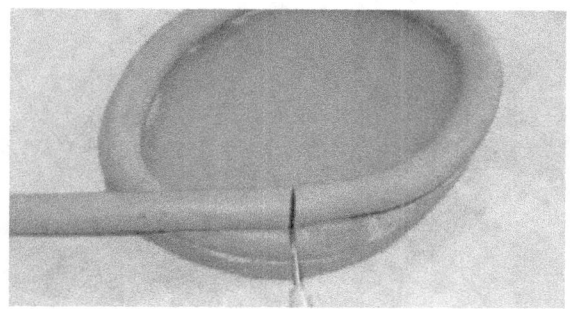

6. Once you are done with the above procedure, use your fingers to blend in the joints with the base. This way, you wouldn't see any ridges or extra spacing. You could also use a knife or a wooden tool for this. If you are using your hands, your right hand should run across the outer surfaces, while your left supports the coil from the inside.

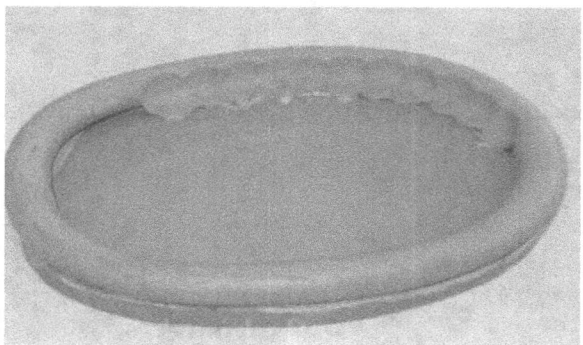

7. Run a rib across the outer surface to make it smooth.

8. Now, set another ring of coil upon the first layer while ensuring that your fingers actively support and press the coil.

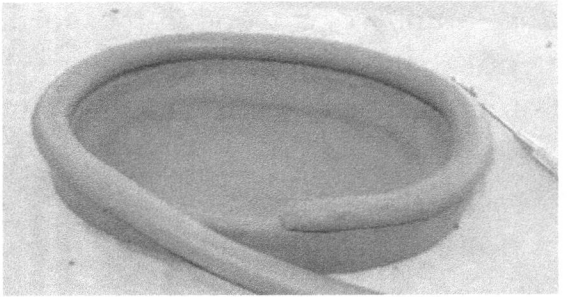

9. Now, blend the second coil into the first base, either with your hands or a wooden tool.

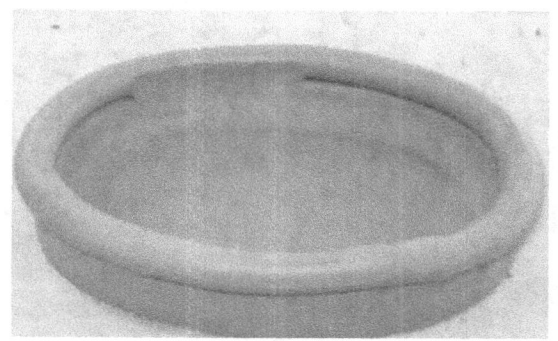

10. Continue to set more layers while ensuring that you stop at intervals to blend the rings properly. If you notice the rings drying out, you could run a wet foam across the surfaces to aid the joinery. You could also add two or three extra layers before getting rid of the creases and lines.

11. Ensure that the point where you trim off the excess coils isn't directly on top of each other. Trim the excesses at different points so that the structure is not weakened.

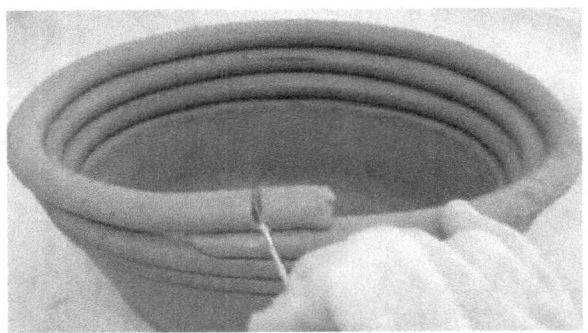

12. Also, as you add more coils, ensure that you add longer coils. This technique will help you get a wider mouth for your pot. As you add the longer coils, ensure that you close up the ridges both inside and outside.

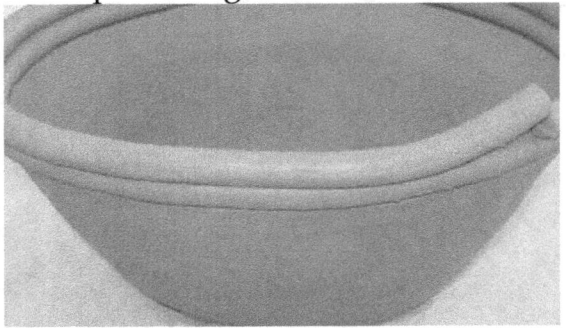

13. If you are making a big pot, you could stop after building the rings up to a point so that it would be strengthened enough to carry the other strings. Doing that will also prevent the structure from crumbling or falling in. To close up the pot, add one final ring. As for

this last ring, you could choose not to blend it with the other rings.

You could also decide to pinch the coils along the length to create a nice pattern.

The finished post should look like the one illustrated in the picture below.

14. Shape the pot's walls to the exact design and structure you want your finished pot to have by working with a paddle.

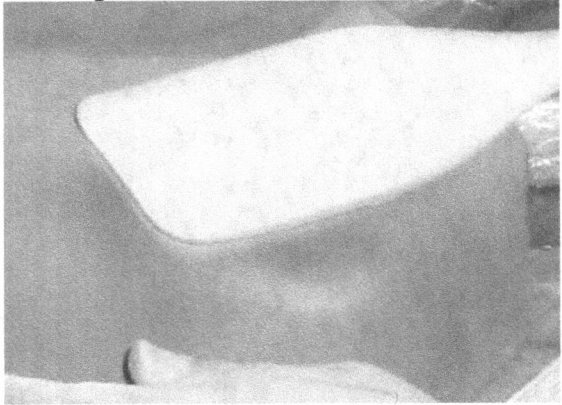

15. Dry the molded pot by placing a plastic covering on top of it.

16. Below are a couple of other illustrations of designs you can choose to work with.

Handbuilt Pinch Pot Hedgehog

Tools and Supplies

- Lump of clay
- Scoring tool
- Pin tool
- Slip
- Clay knife

Procedures

1. Mold your clay lump into round balls, with each one having an approximate weight of about 1/2-pounds.

2. Secure one of the two balls in your left hand, and then use your right thumb to create an opening in the middle by pushing it through the mass. Ensure that your thumb doesn't come out through the other side, though. At least, a base of about 1/4-inch thickness should be left.

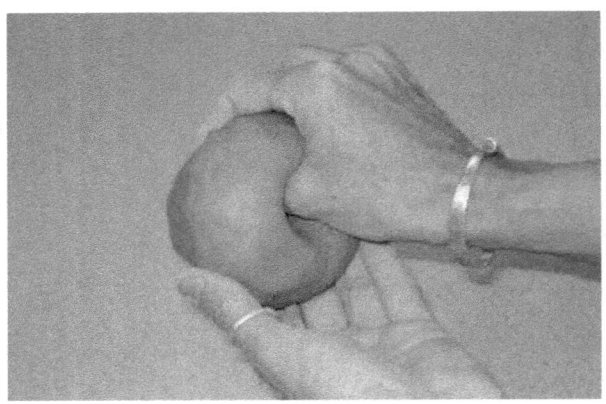

3. From the hole you made, slowly and firmly press the sides so that the hole gets even wider and bigger. Start from where your thumb touches the sides while using your left hand to roll it about the crevices of your palm. From the sides, move to the edges to ensure uniformity in the pattern of your project. Now, repeat the

procedure above and the one described here for the other ball of clay.

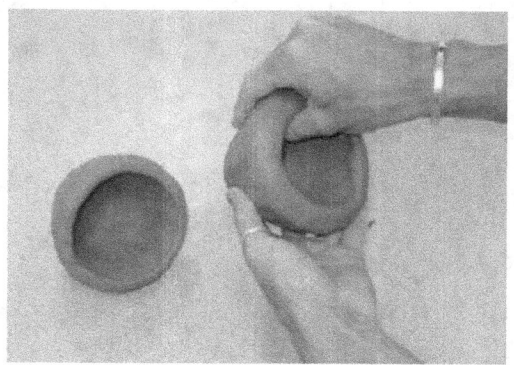

4. After crafting both balls, score the edges with a pin-mouth tool on all the edges. This way, you get a wavy pattern on the edges.

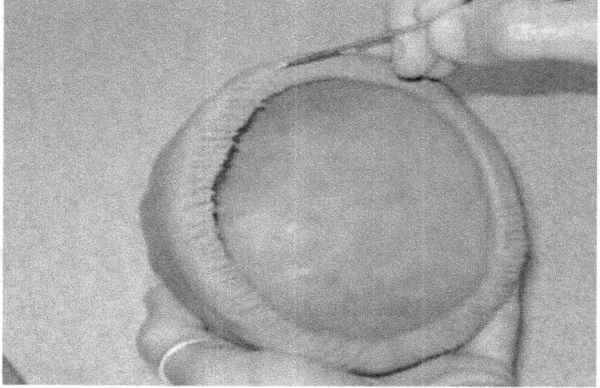

5. Pick one of the pots and then generously add slip to it.

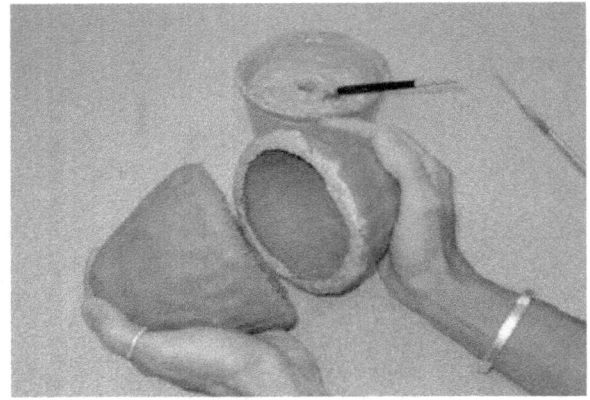

6. Now, join the pots together at their edges. In case of any non-uniform edges, you could use a scraping tool to cut off the excesses. Then, to see to it that the pots become one piece, run your thumbs across the seams to blend their clay bodies.

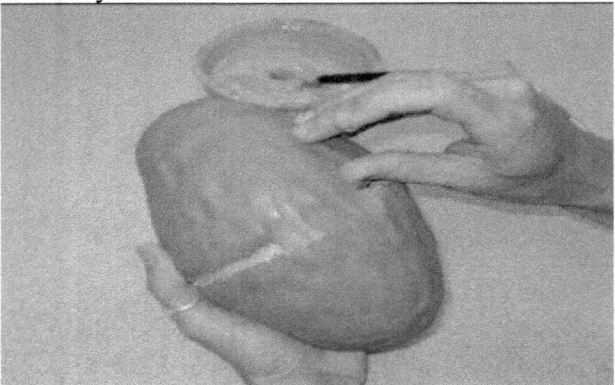

7. Once the two pots have been successfully joined into one, you can roll them across a board to get them into the shape you want them to be in. All you just need to do is roll and press your fingers around certain edges.

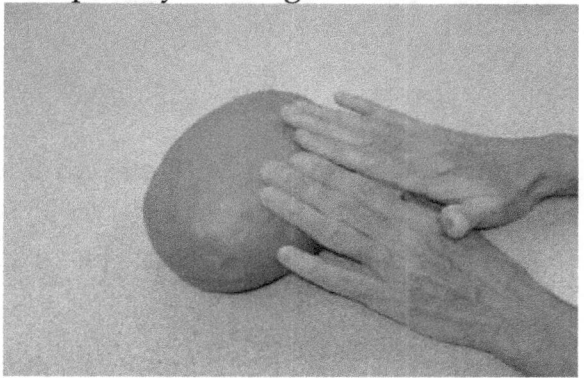

8. To form the hedgehog's head, cut out another lump of clay and form a smaller pinch pot by employing the procedures in numbers 2 and 3 described above. Fix the head to the body made from the two pots above, using the procedures described in steps 4 and 5 above.

9. Add the legs and feet of the hedgehog. Ensure to continue with the slipping and scoring procedures.

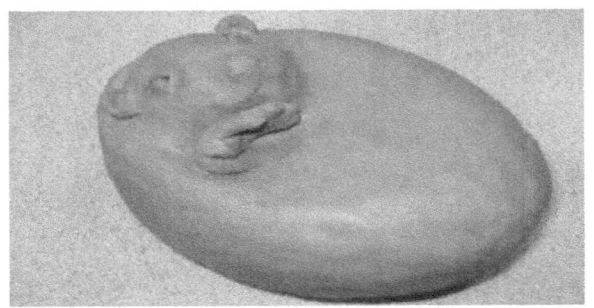

10. For the hedgehog's spines, cut out smaller bits of clay from the lump and roll them into long worm-like coils. The coils should be about 1/2-inches long.

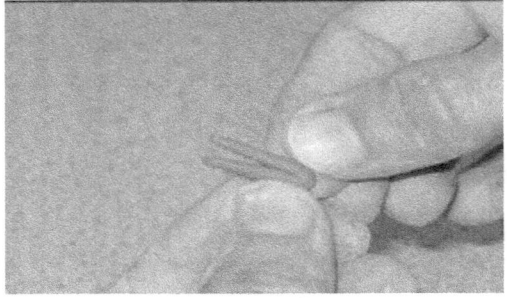

11. Fold the coils into two, and then press the apex of the fold onto the body while ensuring that you press it firmly as you work.

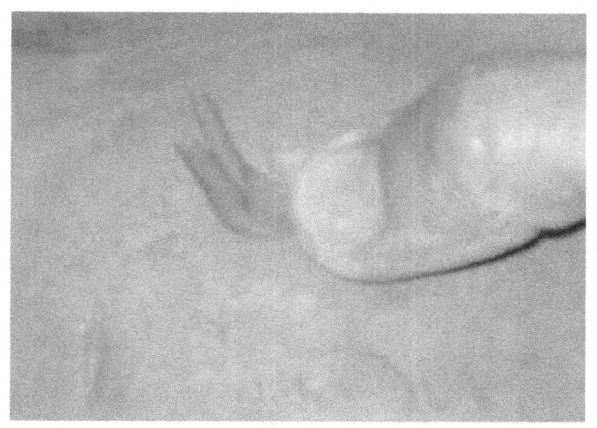

12. Before you fire your clay project, you will need to cut out a hole at the bottom that will serve as a passageway for air while having it dried. You should also ensure that you create another passageway between the head of the hedgehog and the body.

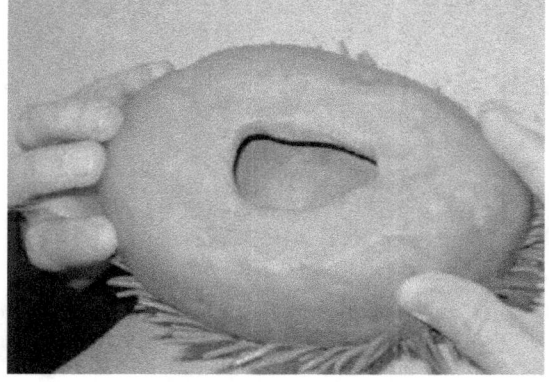

13. To dry the hedgehog, cover it with a plastic covering.

14. While firing your project in the kiln, ensure that you use the high-firing technique so that the spines do not come out being too weak.

Handbuilt Slab Water Font

Tools and Supplies

- Lump of clay
- Rib
- Miter
- Scoring tool
- Clay knife

- Scalloping tool
- Project template
- Wooden platform
- Eggshells for glazing

Procedures

1. Roll out a lump of clay into a slab about 1/4-inches thick hours before you begin this project. When you are done, set the slab on a wooden platform and then cover it with a plastic covering to harden up a little.

2. Cut the slab into the desired size by pressing a template to the surface.

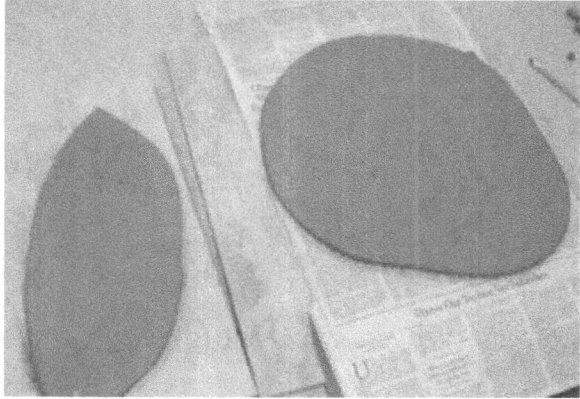

3. Keep the surface of the slab regular by running a rib across it.

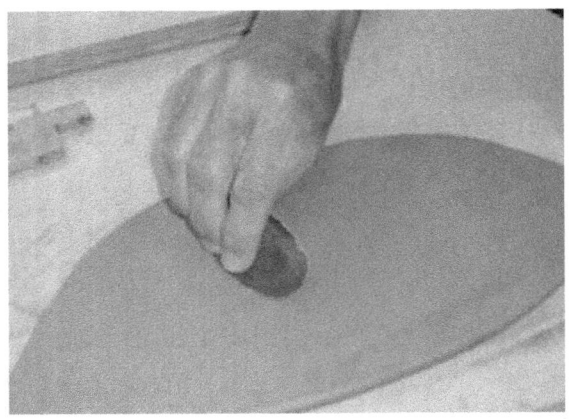

4. Keep the edges of the slab beveled to an angle of thirty degrees with a miter.

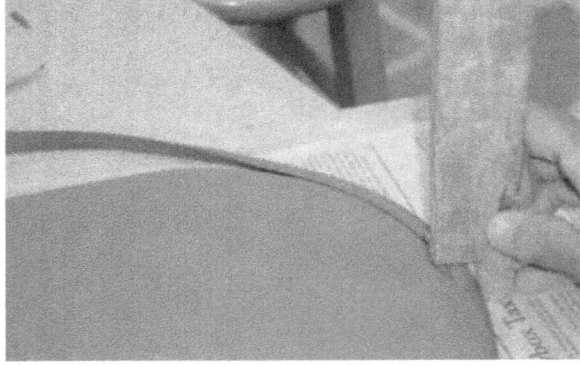

5. Bevel the edge where you would add the second slab.

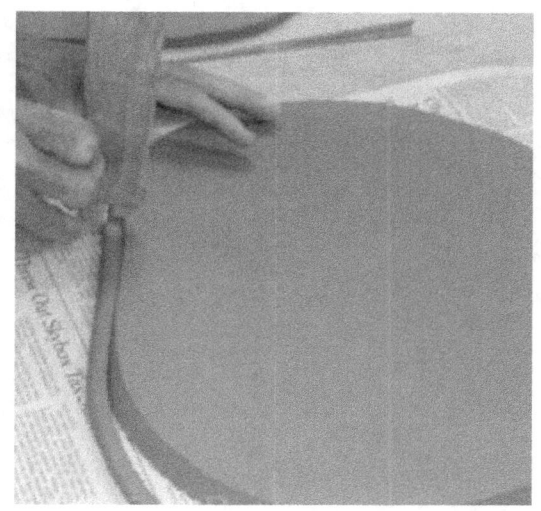

6. Miter the edges of the other slab at one of its edges.

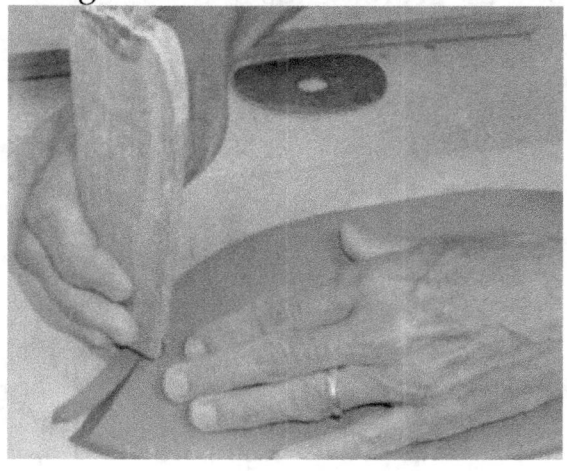

7. Score the edges you beveled in steps 4, 5, and 6.

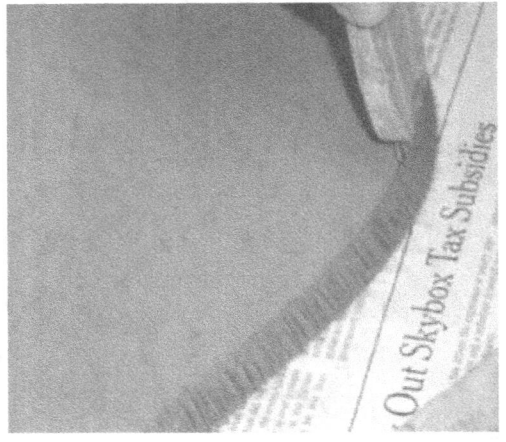

8. Add slip to the scored ends of the slabs.

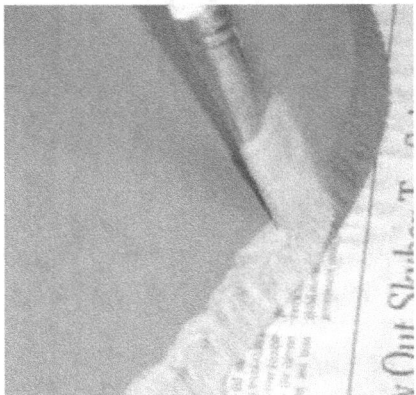

9. Fix the scored end of the first slab to the scored end of the second slab.

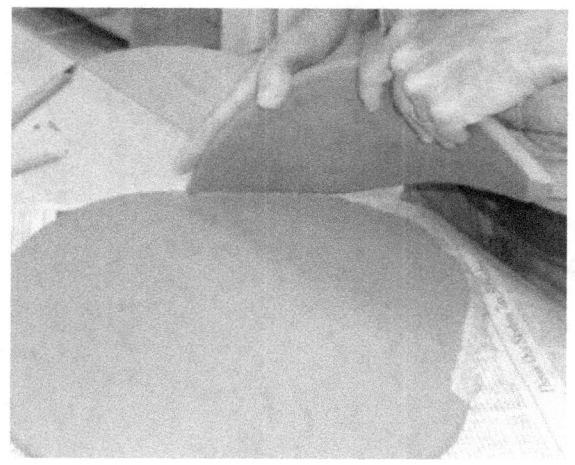

10. Ensure that the manner with which you fix the second slab is uniform. You can then proceed to alter the curves with your fingers after placement.

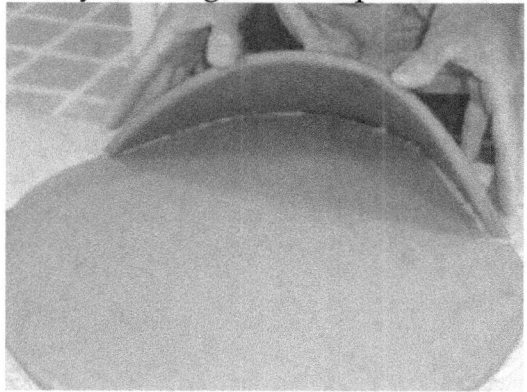

11. Support the point where the two slabs meet with coils of clay.

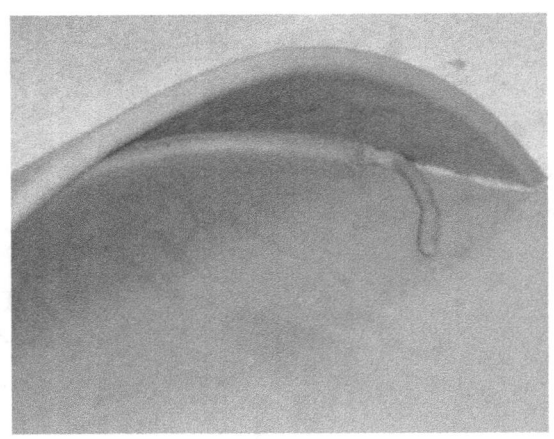

12. Finish the joinery by smoothing the coils with the body of either of the slabs. What you finally get should look like the one below.

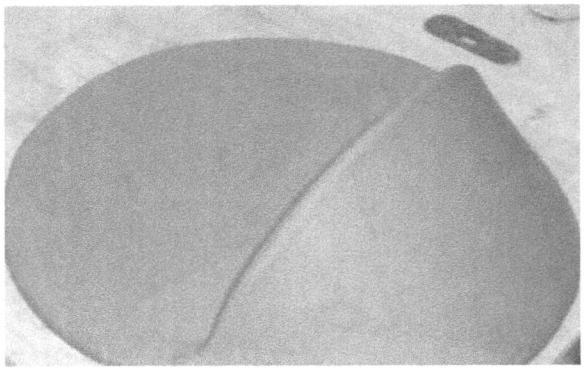

13. You could use a knife to cut out waves at the base.

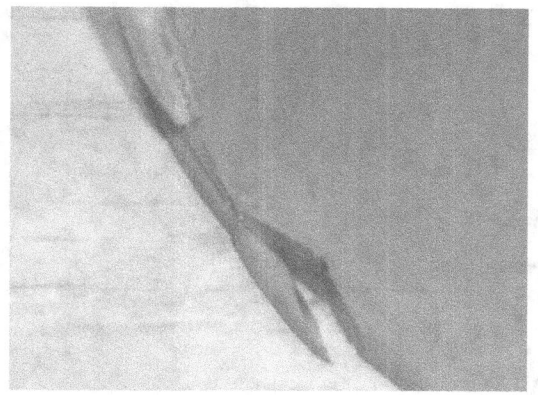

14. Mark points on the edges of the upper slab for scalloping.

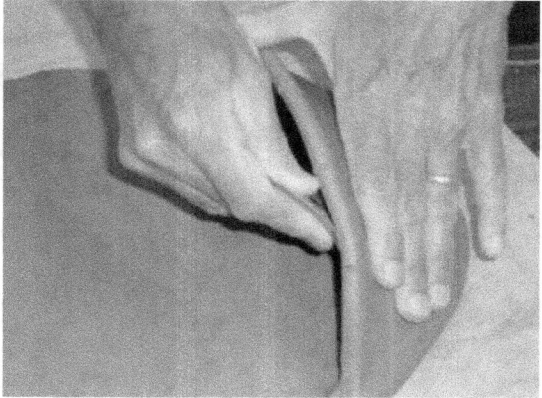

15. Ensure that your scalloping techniques fetch you something that is really defined and neatly curved.

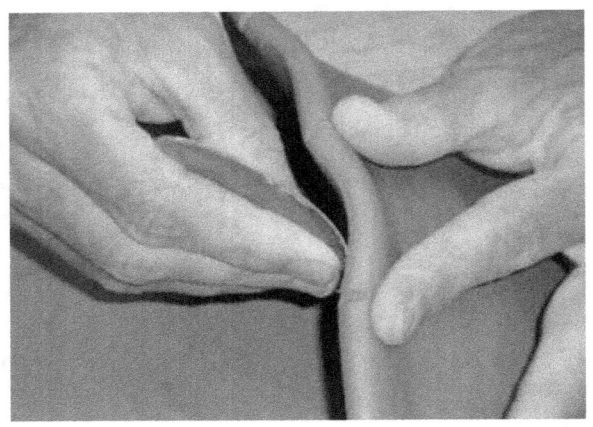

16. Push the rim outwards until you get it in your preferred angle.

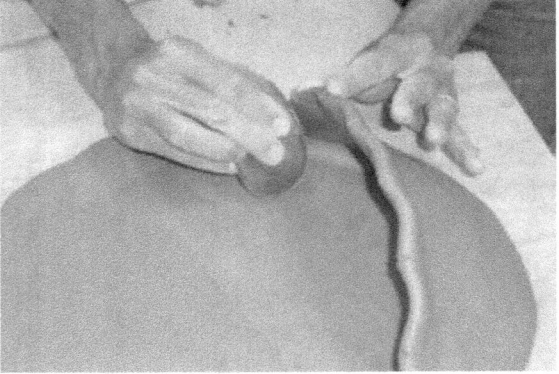

17. Continue scalloping the rim along its length.

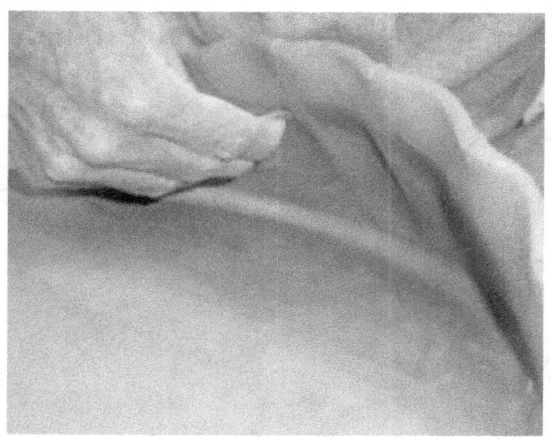

18. As you scallop, ensure that one hand supports your moves at the exterior surface, as shown below.

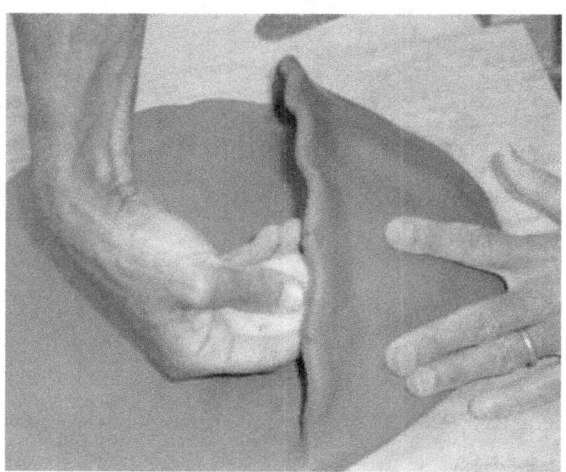

19. Keep your scalloped edges more pronounced with a scalloping tool.

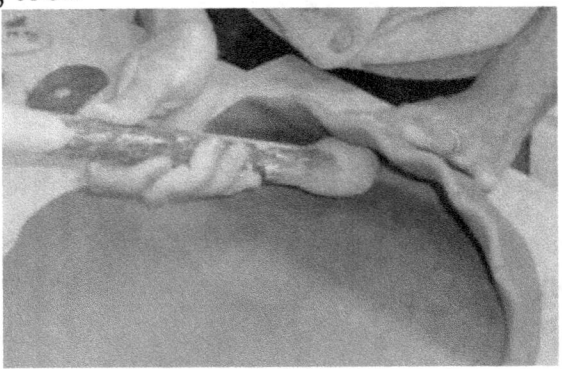

20. The front view of your project should look like the one shown below.

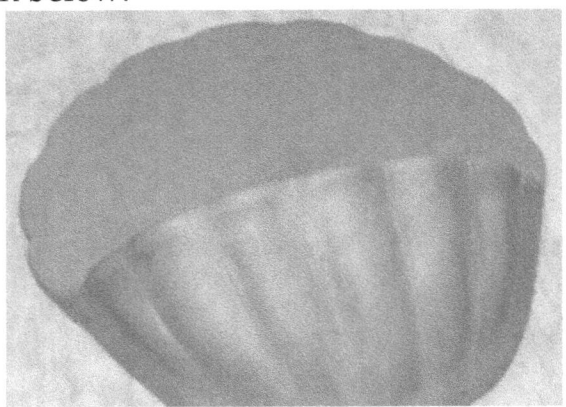

21. The upper view of your project should look like the one shown below.

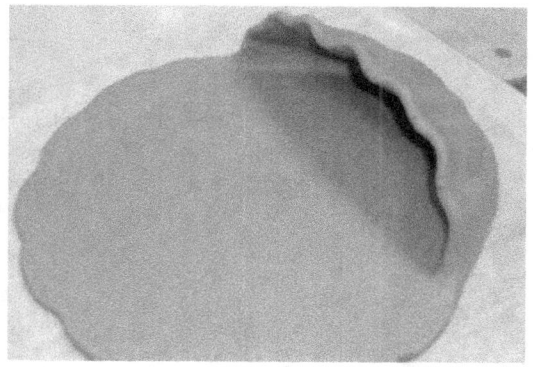

22. Curve out the pattern of a leaf on the base by employing a marking tool. You could use any tool with a sharp edge, though.

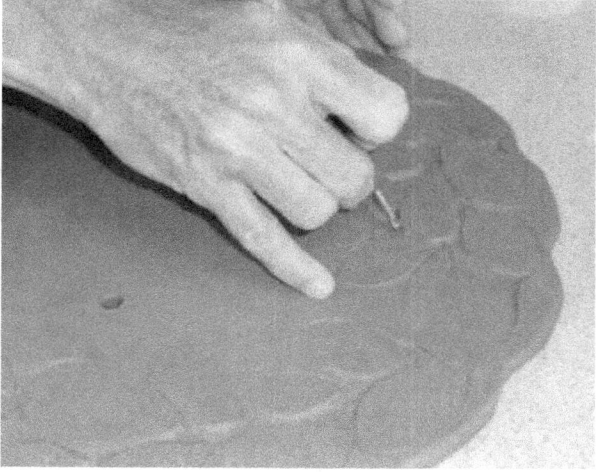

23. Cut out bits of clay in the base to make holes.

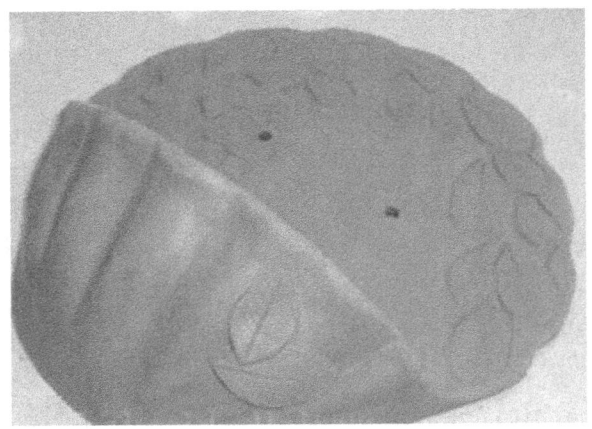

24. In the illustration shown below, the emblem of a cross was inscribed on the surface. You could work with another design if you wish.

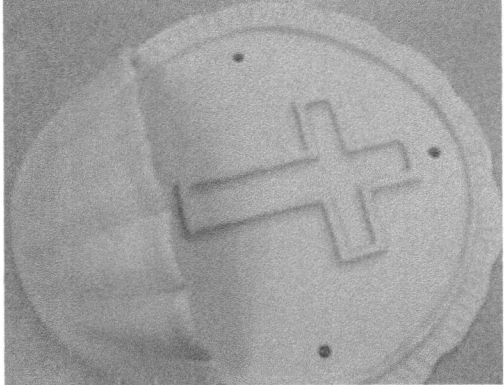

25. Now, you can proceed to glaze your project. The glaze used here is eggshell.

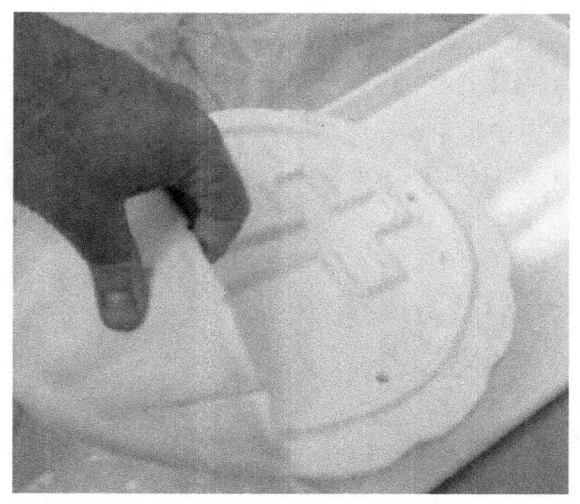

26. Finish the project with a water font. The result should have the outlook of the illustration below.

Wheel Thrown Hookah Head

Tools and Supplies

- Clay lump
- A pair of the caliper
- Smoothing tool
- Pin-mouthed tool
- Decorating disks
- Plastic sheaths
- 1/4-inch clay punch tool

Procedures

1. Start by throwing clay of about 1 3/4-lb into the shape you desire to have the hookah in. Here, the dimensions for the hookah are 4 1/2-inches in width and 4-inches in height. The four inches do not include the neck of the hookah's bottom.

2. As you throw the hookah, ensure that there's a hole left at the bottom, just like you would have in a planting pot.

3. You should also work with a pair of calipers to ensure that you have the hookah crafted out at the right dimensions.

4. Use a torch or dryer to harden the thrown hookah before you move on to the next step.

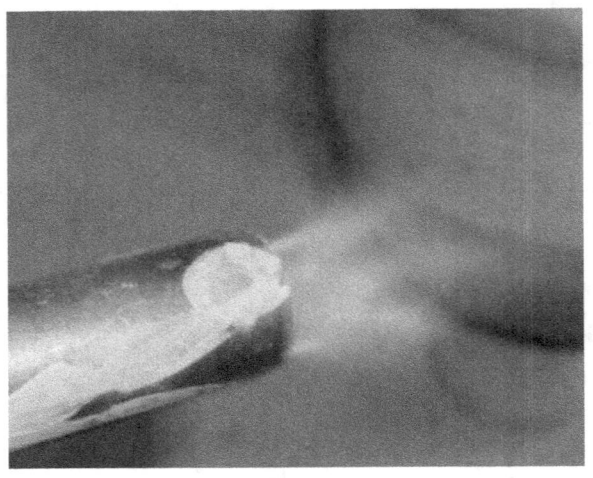

5. To make the top of the hookah, you would need a clay lump of about 1/2-lb weight. It also should have a thickness of about 1/4-inches. Having two wheels would benefit you as you would throw the bowl on one and the base on another.

6. Trim the top of the hookah with a pin-mouthed tool.

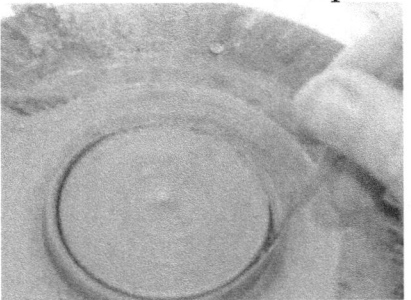

7. Remove the top of the hookah from the platform on which you threw it.

8. Set the top of the hookah on the mouth of the body.

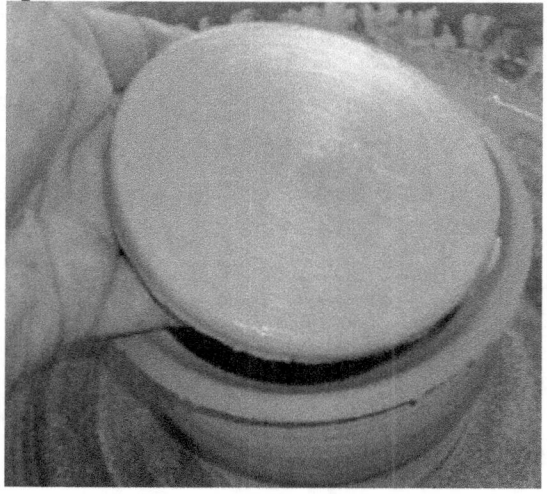

9. To create a passageway for air to escape from the hookah, drill a hole through the top with a pin-mouthed tool.

10. Blend the body of the hookah to that of the top by using your fingers or a wooden tool. Blend them until they have the required depth. Before you work on the top of the hookah, ensure that you use a torch to get it hardened a bit. As you go through that process, ensure that the hole you made in step 9 doesn't disappear.

11. Use a pair of calipers to measure the other dimensions. This way, you can check to see that you are in line with whatever template or guide you are following.

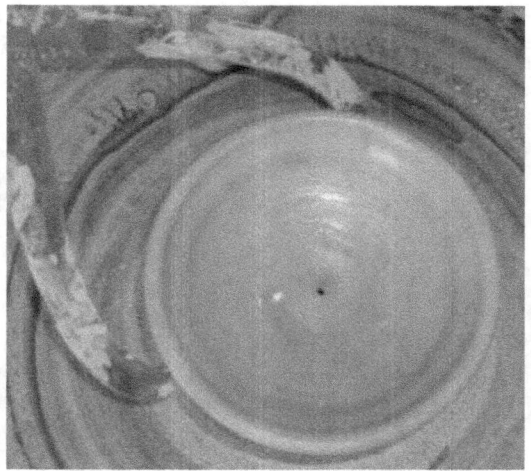

12. Run a smoothing tool across the sides of the hookah's body to get it into the required shape.

13. Dry your project by covering it with a plastic sheath to get it hardened.

14. Proceed to use a decorating disk to mark out the points where you wish to drill holes.

15. To drill the holes, you could make use of 1/4-inch clay hole punching tools.

16. Turn the bowl upside down so that you can work on its bottom.

17. Trim the bottom of the hookah until you get a rounded structure. As you go through the trimming

process, ensure that you spray the hookah with water to keep it moist.

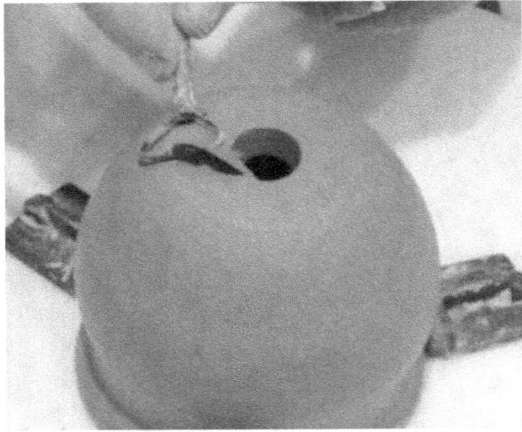

18. Throw the base neck of the hookah.

19. Use a pair of calipers to ensure that the neck of the base is fitted to the right diameter. If the clay is wet, you could work with a dimension of 30mm.

20. Fix the base to the bottom of the hookah bowl.

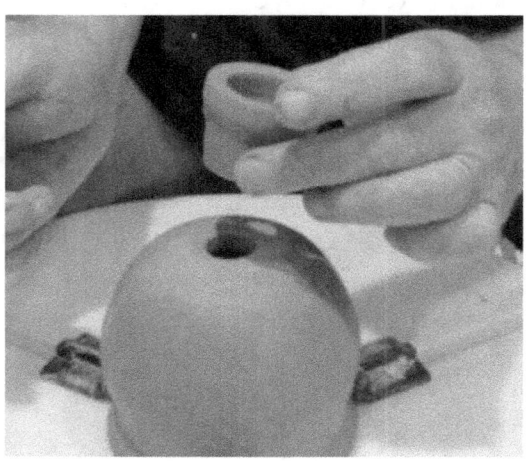

21. While turning the body of the hookah, place the neck base at the bottom of the hookah. Then, use a coil of clay to aid a proper attachment of the neck to the body.

22. As you integrate the two components, it should get to a point where the coil disappears. Use the illustration given below as a guide.

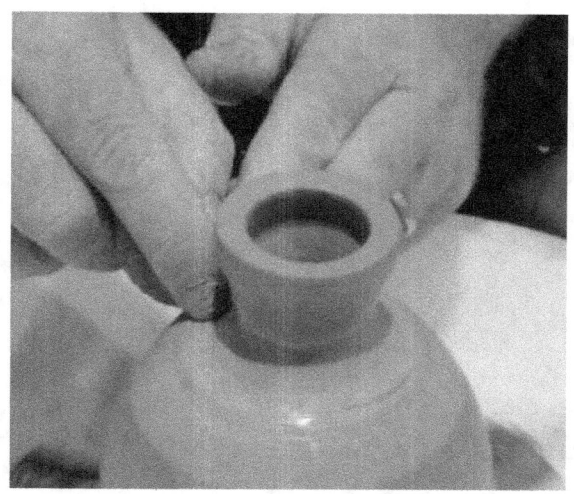

23. Cover the hookah with a plastic sheet so that it can dry.

24. Glaze the project all over with the aid of a wet pipe cleaning tool.

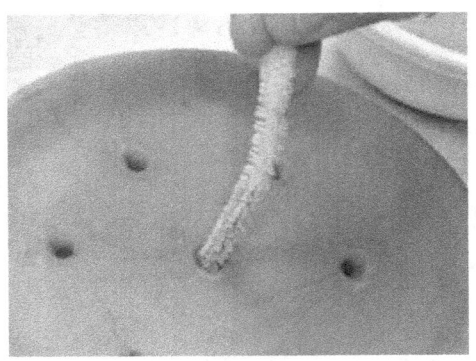

25. Set the glazed hookah in a kiln to have it fired to a temperature of about 2,200 degrees.

26. The result of the hookah should look like the one illustrated below.

Pottery Clay Tray

Tools and Supplies

- Slab of 1/4-inches clay
- Pinning tool
- Window pipe
- Stamps
- Rolling Pin
- Leaves
- Newspaper
- Lubricant
- Piece of wood with rounded base corners

- 2 1/2-inches thick foam that is larger than the size of your tray

Procedures

1. Roll the clay lump to a flat slab of about 1/4-inches thickness using a rolling pin or a slab rolling device.

2. Trim the clay into the dimensions that you need your tray to be in. What you get should be rectangular.

3. Set the flattened piece of clay on a sheet of newspaper.

4. Run a window pipe across the surface of the newspaper to get it regular and smooth.

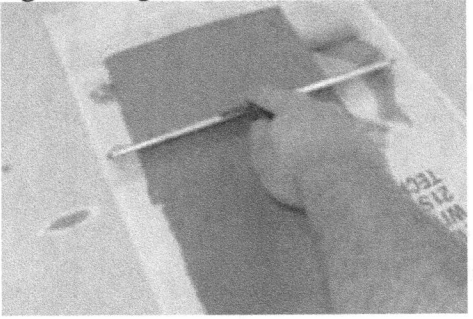

5. Use a piece of wood as a guide in marking points for the inner parts of the clay tray.

6. Set the leaves you got to the middle square of the tray, and then use a rolling pin to press them in place.

7. Use a stamp to embellish the tray's rims. You could also use any other decorating tool for this.

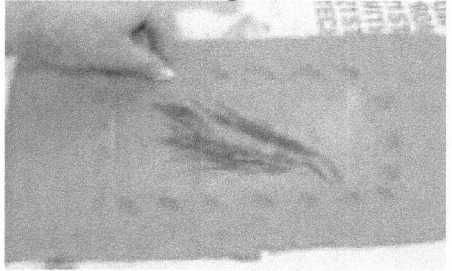

8. Trim the clay slab about an inch away from the markings made in step 5. Ensure that the trimmings are about half an inch away from the markings.

9. Shift the slab to the foam with the aid of the newspaper it was laid upon.

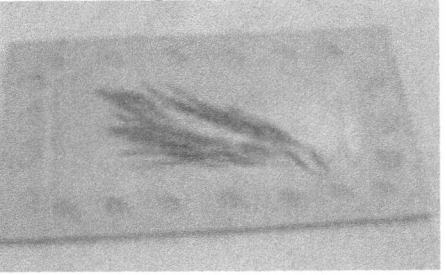

10. Set the piece of wood in the middle of the clay. Since the outer dimensions of the clay slab are about eight inches by twelve inches, the wooden piece should be about six inches by ten inches. The side of the wood that you are to place on the clay also should have been greased beforehand.

11. Press the wooden piece into the slab until the clay's rime is at the right angle. Once that is done, you can stop applying pressure to the wooden piece.

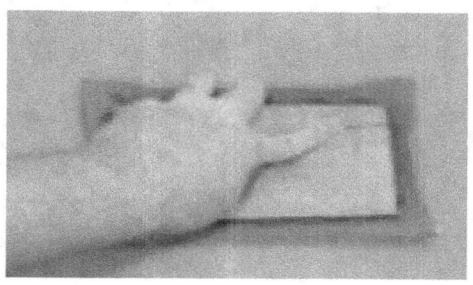

12. To take the wooden piece off, use a pin tool to lift one of the corners gently.

13. Use a plastic sheath to cover the tray so that it can dry.

14. Glaze the tray before proceeding to fire it with the cone 6 firing technique.

15. You can then fix glass shards to the project when you are done.

Wheel Thrown Mug

Tools and Supplies

- Clay lump
- Throwing wheel
- Rib
- Ruler
- Trimming tool
- Template for mug design
- Pencil or scribe tool

Procedures

1. Carve out about 1 3/4-lb of clay from the main slab.

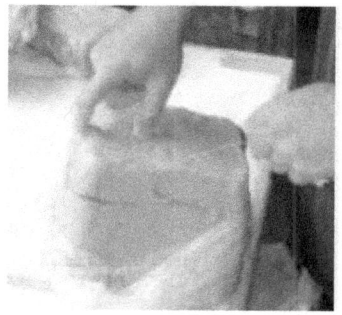

2. Press the clay into a solid lump.

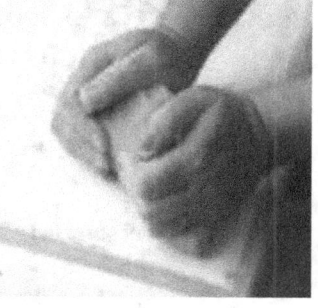

3. Set the lump on a throwing wheel.

4. Mold up the clay at the center.

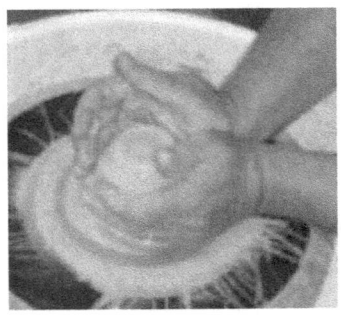

5. Now, press the clay at the top so that the surface becomes wide enough for you to work on. Ensure that your fingers work at the top during this step.

6. Apply more pressure at the center so that you get a groove. Once the groove is formed at the center, the walls would instantly form around it. Use your fingers to press the walls into the dimensions that you want to work with.

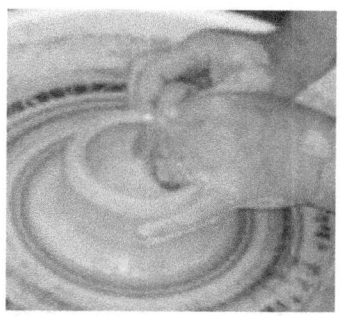

7. Work your fingers from the bottom to the top to uniformly distribute the clay across the length. The technique will also ensure that the walls get higher.

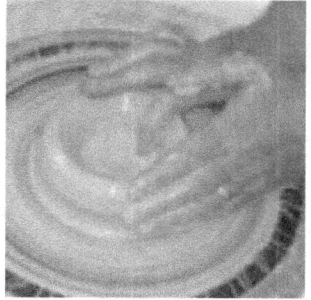

8. Continue to work your fingers across the length of the walls until you get the required dimensions.

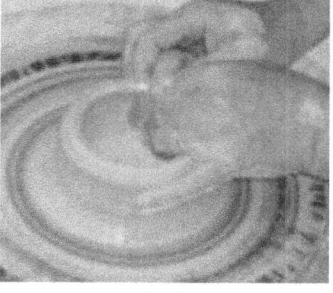

9. Consequently, measure the height that you have worked the walls to.

10. You should also measure the breadth of the opening.

11. Use a rib to make the walls smooth and regular.

12. The thrown mug should look like the one in the illustration below.

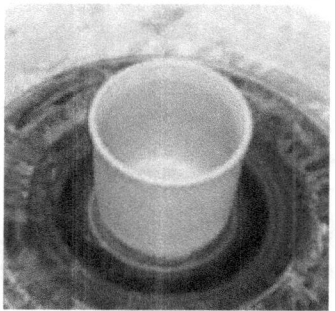

13. Turn the clay mug upside down so that you can trim off the excesses at the ends.

14. Trim the ends of the clay until you get the required dimensions.

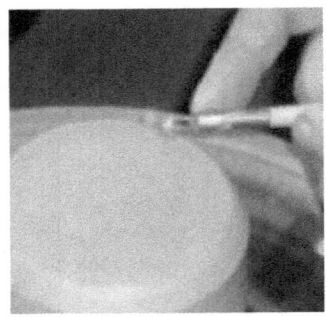

15. The final result should look like the one illustrated below.

16. Roll out a handle from the clay lump

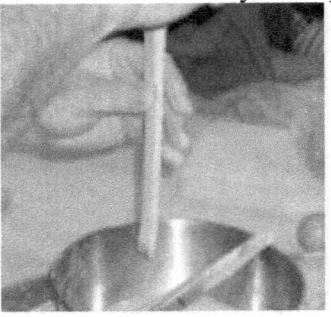

17. Leave the handle to dry a bit or use a dryer to get faster results.

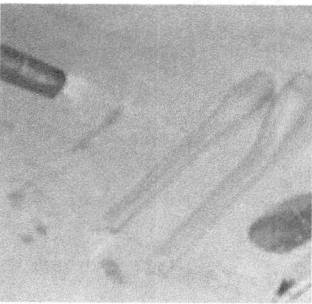

18. Press one end of the handle to the top of the mug.

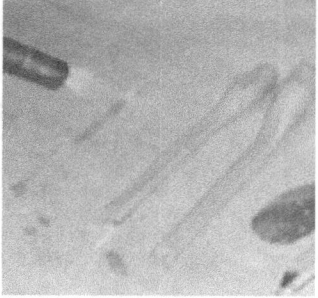

19. Press the other end of the handle to the lower edge of the mug.

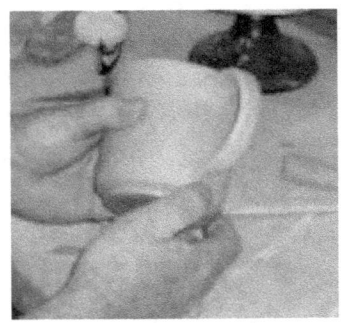

20. Adjust the curve that the handle forms into the regular mug handle.

21. Layout the pattern you want to make across the surface of the mug.

22. Trace out the paper template on the mug with a pencil.

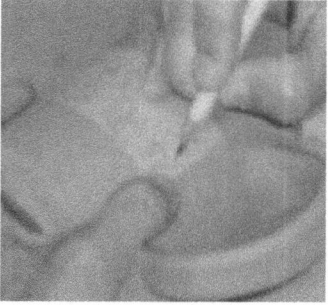

23. Bisque the mug using cone 6.

24. Glaze the bottom ridge of the mug.

25. Highlight the traced lines with an underglaze (of color and decoration applied to a piece) technique.

26. You can now proceed to fire your mug in a kiln.

27. The finished mug should look closely like the one illustrated below.

Handbuilt Slab Shoe

Tools and Supplies

- Scissors
- Rolling pin

- Miter or a 45-degree beveling tool
- Wooden tool
- Clay knife
- Pin tool
- Sponge
- Flexible rib
- Pliable clay

Procedures

1. Cut out templates for your shoe using paper.

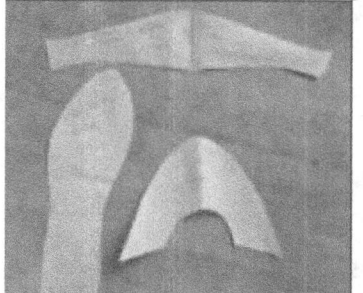

2. Use a rolling pin to roll a clay lump into a flattened sheet. The sheet should be about 1/4-inches thick.
3. Place the templates on the clay slab, and then cut out the outlines with a clay knife.

4. Use a miter to fuse the parts. The parts should be at an angle of 45-degrees to each other.

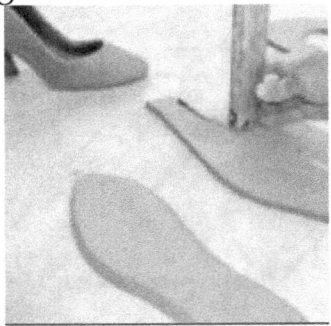

5. Close the beveled edges.

6. Cut out the sole of the shoe at the center of the slab.

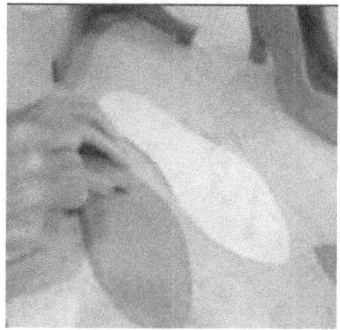

7. Score the points where the parts are to be fused.

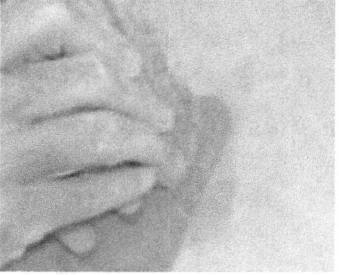

Apply slip to the scored edges.

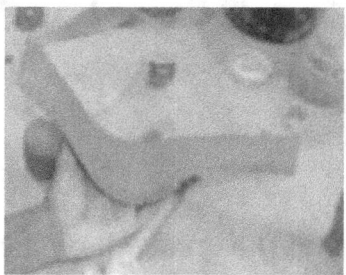

8. Fix the slab for the heel to the scored edges. If the slab is a bit too rigid, ensure that you wrap it gently about

the edges of the sole. You could also make things easy by cutting the sole into two.

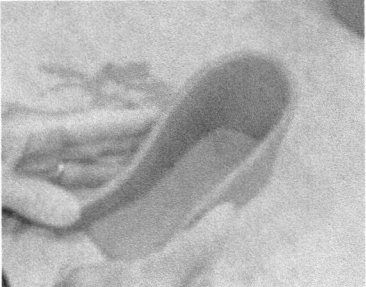

P.S: If you plan on cutting the sole, ensure that the length of the heel goes beyond the sole's length so that you do not have issues merging the other half back.

9. Blend the edges of the heel to that of the sole with your fingers.

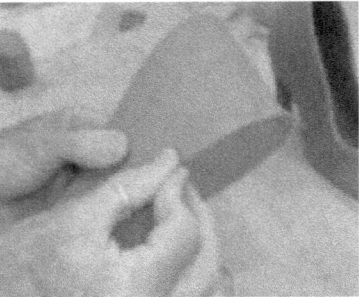

To strengthen the joint, run a coil of clay around it at the interior edges.

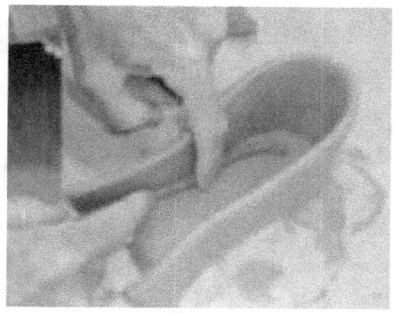

10. Use your fingers to blend the coil in with the sole and the heel.

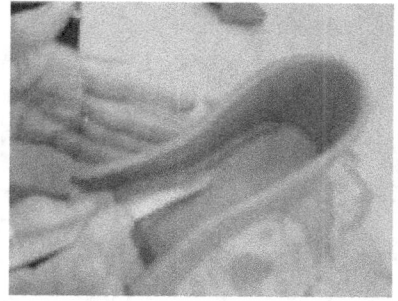

11. Run a smoothing tool across the joined edges.

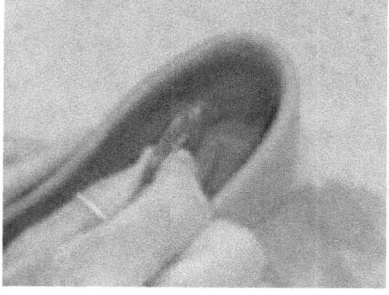

12. Use a rib to incline the heel to the right shape and angle.

13. Work with a template while cutting out a base for the heel.

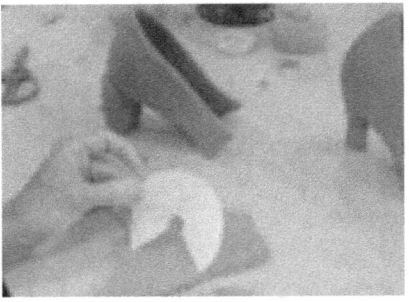

14. Cut out the template's outline on the clay slab for the heel's base, and then score the edges.

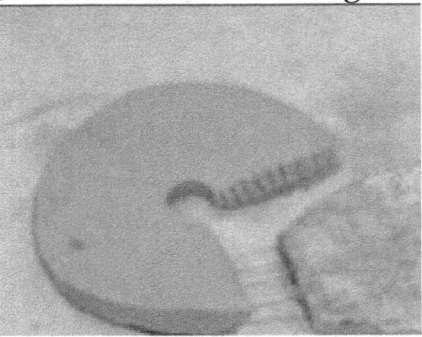

15. Mark out the point where the heel's base is to be fixed at the back of the shoe.

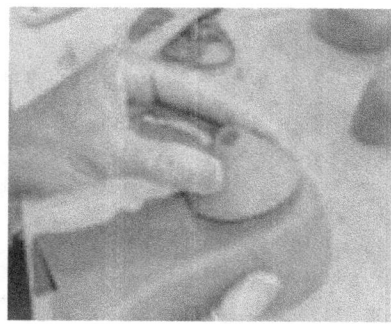

16. After adding slip to the edges of the heel's base, score it, and then fix it to the heel. To make the joint stronger, add a coil to the joinery areas and then blend them in.

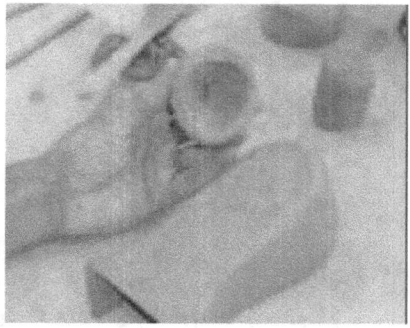

17. Place your half-finished project next to a completed shoe.

18. Work on a lump of clay until it is about 1/8-inches thin. Then, work it out into the shape of a rectangle. As for the length, make it a few inches longer than what you plan to work with.

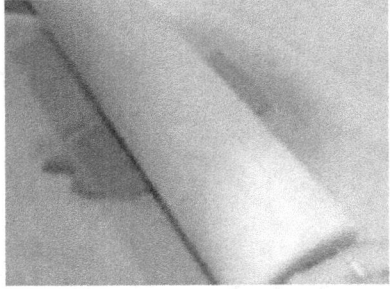

19. Miter the alternate ends of the rectangular clay lump, and then roll it around the length of a wooden spoon. Slip, score, and blend it once you are done.

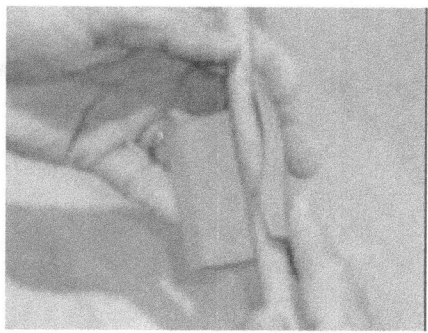

20. Attach the scored tube to the bottom of the heel.

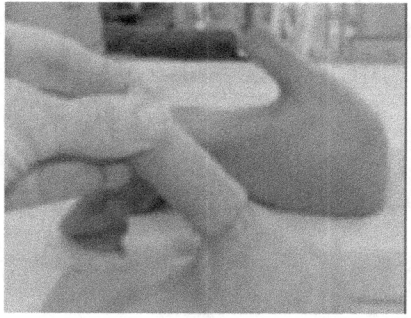

21. Use a coil of clay to support the edges. When you are done, blend the coil with the body of the shoe.

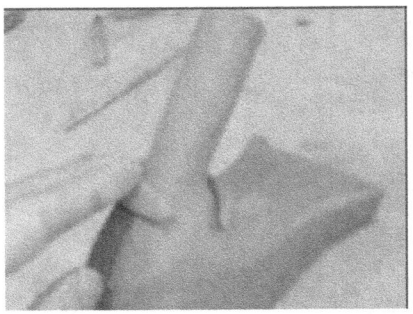

22. Trim the tube to the desired height. Ensure that the height you trim it to matches the base of the toe's clay slab for a balanced effect! Since the tube is hollow, ensure that you make a hole through it so that there's a passageway for air to escape through.

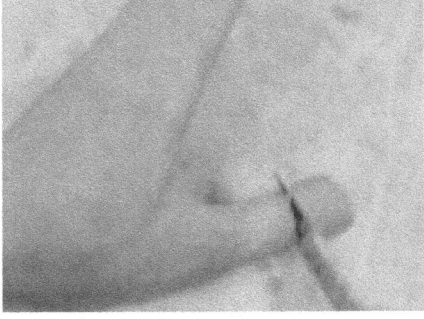

23. Now, join the top of the toe's slab to the sole's toe by using the mitering, scoring, and slipping techniques. Then, you could go on to support the joined areas by passing a coil through them.

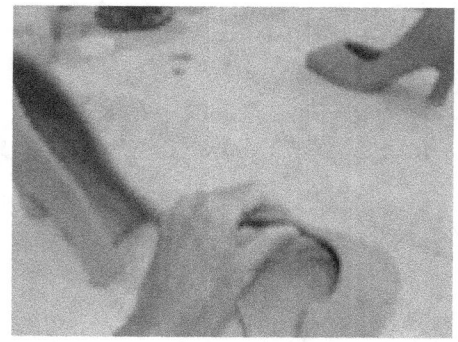

24. Trim off the excess clay.

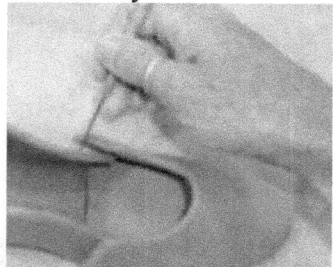

25. Trim off the excess clay on the bevel too.

26. Score and apply slip on all of the edges.

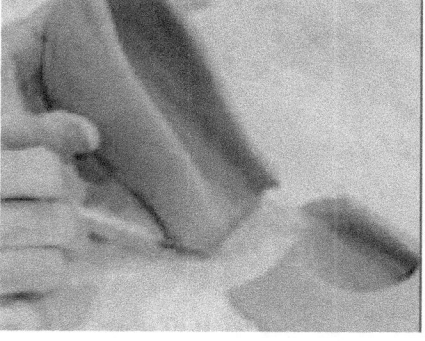

27. Reinforce the joined areas with coils, and then blend them with the rest of the body.

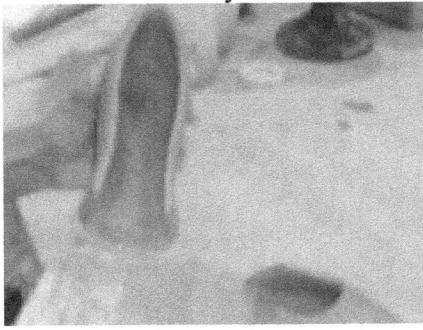

28. Embellish the shoe by working with very thin pieces of the slab. The illustration below shows a couple of designs that you could work with.

29. The finished shoes should look like the one shown in the illustration below.

Wheel Thrown Chicken Coop Waterer

Tools and Supplies

- Throwing wheel
- Rib
- Clay knife
- Pin tool
- Clay lump

Procedures

1. Throw in a lump of clay of about 6-lbs weight on the throwing wheel.

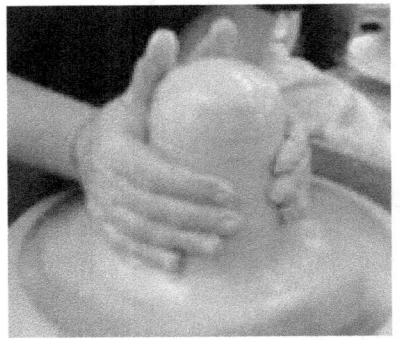

2. Mold the clay at the center of the wheel.

3. Press the lump down by working your fingers at the top of the lump. You would need to apply enough pressure to get this result.

4. Apply more pressure at the center of the clay lump so that a hole is formed. However, you should leave about 3/8-inches of clay at the bottom.

5. Work your fingers sideways so that walls are formed around the central hole. The width of the formed hole should be about six inches wide.

6. Proceed to work your fingers up the walls to increase their height.

7. To increase the height of the walls some more, continue to work your fingers upwards. One hand should work its way through the inner walls while the other hand braces the wall from the outer side.

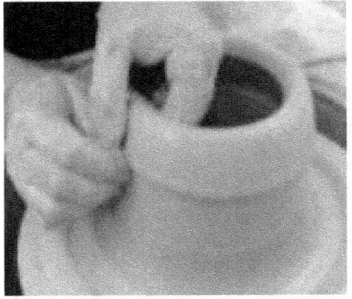

8. The last series of work you make through the walls will be to make the walls uniform.

9. Since the top of the bowl would have thickened due to the upward working of your hands, you will need to press it into a neat curve.

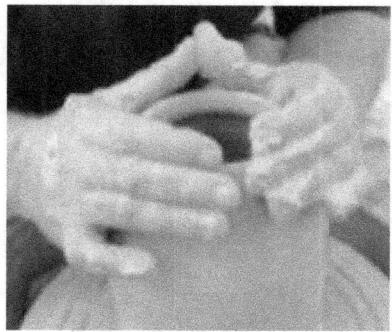

10. Now, use your two hands to press the sides of the mouth into a thinner layer, and then pull it up even more.

11. Mold the walls of the waterer into the shape you desire, and as you do that, ensure that you use both hands to press against the walls.

12. Fold in the walls of the neck towards the mid-line of the waterer.

13. Continue to give shape to the neck so that there is a clear bridge between the neck and the body.

14. After defining the neck, use a rib to add more effect to the shape of the waterer's body.

15. Reduce the mouth of the waterer until it's just wide enough for one of your fingers to run through.

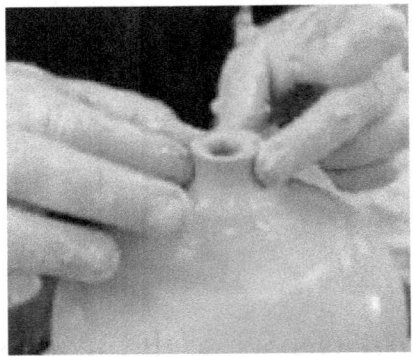

16. Mold out the outline of the waterer's knob.

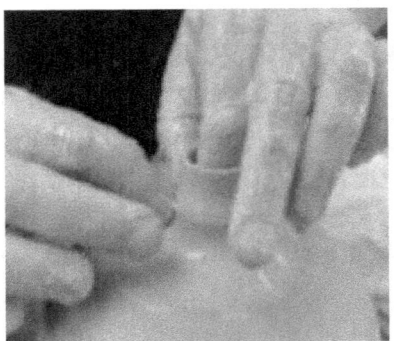

17. Now, completely close up the mouth of the waterer.

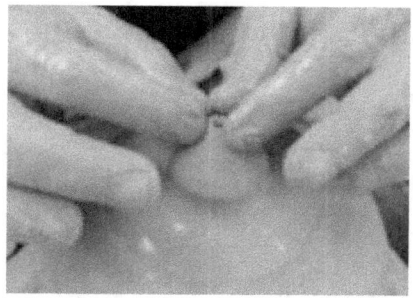

18. Press a bit of clay to the mouth to ensure that the hole is closed up. You should get a more defined and thick knob now.

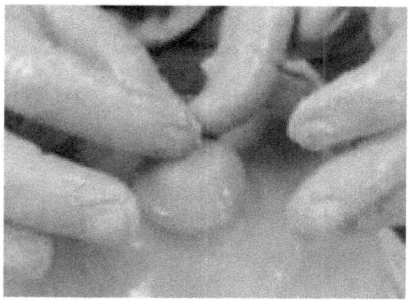

19. Use your fingers to give the knob-like mouth a nice shape, as illustrated below.

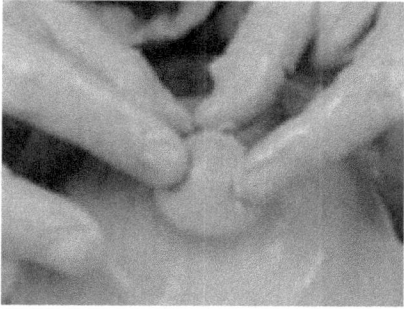

20. Mold out ridges at the bottom of the knob with your fingers.

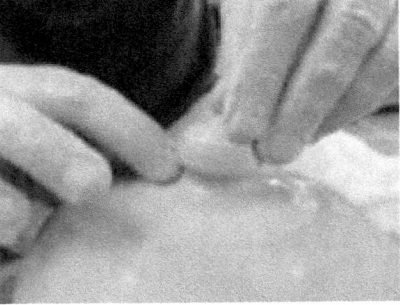

21. Now, to get the walls at the bottom of the waterer at the right density, use a scraping tool or clay knife to cut off the excesses. You should incline your hands at an angle that is inclined towards the mid-line of the waterer.

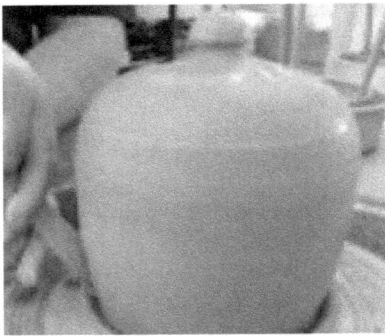

22. Get rid of the excess clay that you scrape off.

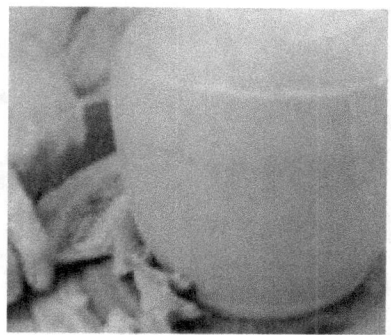

23. Pass a pin-hole tool through one side of the walls of the waterer to create a passageway for air while you dry your project.

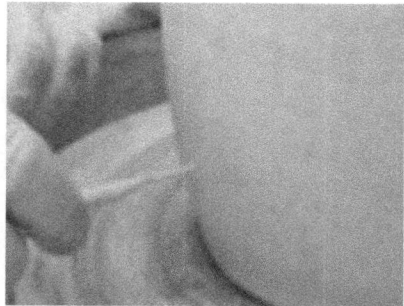

24. When your clay pot has dried a bit, make a slit at a point 3/4" inches from the bottom.

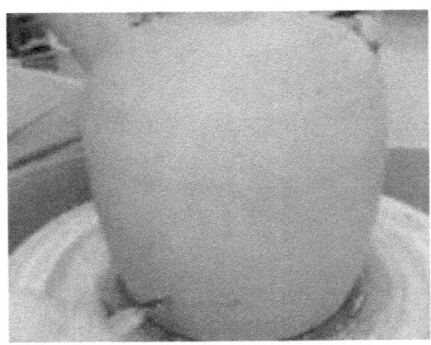

25. Place your fingers along the line of the slit, and then gently push in the upper lip towards the interior of the waterer.

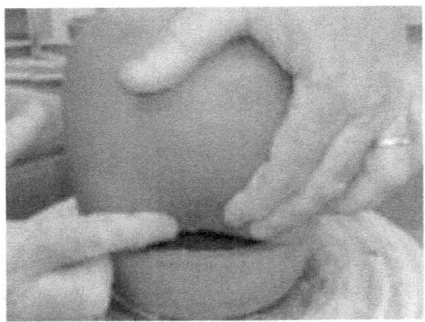

26. Press the upper limb carefully towards the mid-line of the waterer some more until you get a well-defined ridge.

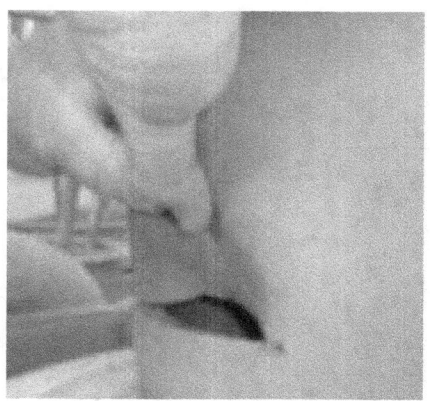

27. Thin the lower lip of the slit, and then push it up to the point that it is well above the upper lip. This way, water wouldn't be able to leak out of the waterer. If the lip is too thin to be stretched upwards, you could work in an extra coil of clay to the outer edge.

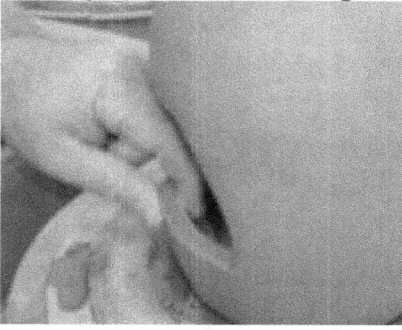

28. Adjust the lower lip to the desired shape. The tip of the bottom should be pointed.

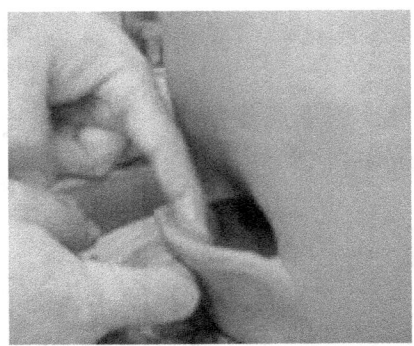

29. You could add another ring to the lower lip to increase the height.

30. Fuse the added coil to the lower lip by pressing the ridges together with your fingers.

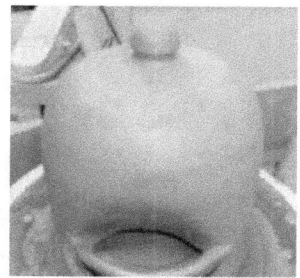

31. When you are done, dry the project with a torch.

32. Your finished project should look like the one shown in the illustration below.

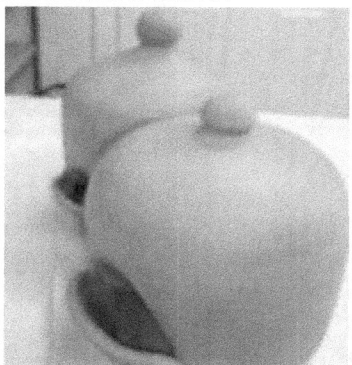

33. When glazing, know that the whole inside of the pot must be glazed for easy cleaning. Spraying the outside and pouring glaze inside is the best way to go about it.

Wheel Thrown Pottery Bowl

Tools and Supplies

- Throw wheel
- Sponge
- Wooden rib
- Metal rib
- Needle tool
- Clay lump

Procedures

1. Mold your clay lump into a square-shaped lump. Then, you could go ahead to make the edges of the lump round by running it across a flat table. The

rounded clay edges will help prevent a scenario where the air is trapped between the wheel and the clay.

2. Grip the square clay lump with the hand you work with the most, and then place it about two centimeters above the center of the throwing wheel. Ensure that you don't let go of the clay lump before it hits the center.

3. The moment the clay hits the center, tap it firmly downwards so that it sticks well to the wheel.

4. Moisten the clay with a damp towel or foam, and then set the throwing wheel's speed from medium to fast.

5. Set your left hand at the left side of the lump and then your right hand at the lump's head. This technique is to help you centralize the clay lump on the wheel. The more pressure you apply to the left side, the taller the lump will be, and the more pressure you apply on top of the lump, the flatter the lump will be. As you continue to centralize the lump, ensure that you continue to dampen the lump.

6. To make the middle of the lump more defined, press the thumbs of your two hands at the center, with the rest of your fingers spread uniformly apart. Continue to dampen your clay even as you get this process done.

7. While getting the bowl to have a well-defined center, you should also ensure that there's enough clay at the

bottom. To measure the thickness of the clay at the bottom, stop the spinning wheel and then pass a pin-mouthed tool through the base. Stop pushing the pin through when you touch the surface of the wheel.

8. Mark the point on the tool where the clay stops with your fingers, and then, pull the tool out. Ensure that the base is about half an inch on the needle. If the base is thicker than 1/2-inches, continue to work at the central spot. Continue to work on the base until you get the required depth.

9. Once you get the pot to the right depth, continue to broaden the mouth. You can place your wheel on medium speed and work up the walls from the center with your hands. To get the pot with an even center, you should work your fingers slowly. If the friction between your hands and the clay increases, consequently moisten your fingers in a bowl of water.

10. Now, proceed to pull the edges of the clay upwards. For this, your throwing wheel should spin slowly. The thumbs of your fingers should be crossed as they would

help you to move in nice rhythms. As you work the clay walls upwards, you should also ensure that your fingers pinch them at intervals. The wall gets thin and tall as you proceed. To prevent the clay walls from breaking up, you should ensure that you moisten your fingers regularly.

11. With your thumbs still crossed above each other, continue to lift the walls. This time, you want the walls of the pot to expand at the outer dimensions, so, you should impress more force on the index finger of your

left hand. You should also moisten your fingers here too.

As you pull up the walls, there's a possibility of the edges becoming uneven. Now, to correct that, reduce the spin of the wheel to the lowest, and then place the thumb and the index finger of your finger at either side of the bowl's edges. Ensure that you do not apply too much force with your fingers.

12. To get rid of the extra moisture from your project, run a foam chip across the interior and exterior walls of the bowl.

Your finished project should look like the illustration below.

Handbuilt Clay Starfish Box

Tools and Supplies

- Rolling pin
- Starfish template
- Scoring tool
- Pencil
- Clay lump
- Clay knife
- Wooden plank
- Sponge

- Foam
- Pin-mouthed tool

Procedures

1. Flatten your lump of clay with a rolling pin or slab rolling device.

2. Use a rib to press in the clay slab and also to make the surface regular.

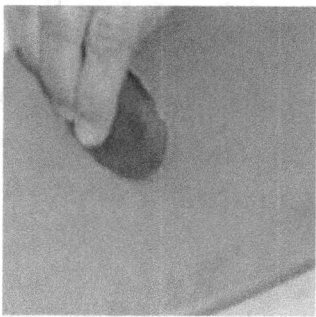

3. Get the template for the starfish ready.

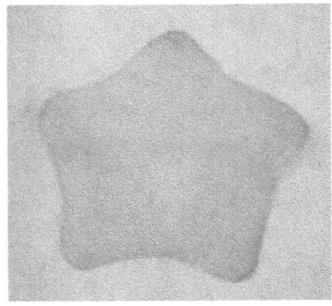

4. Use a pencil to trace out the outline of the starfish on the slab.

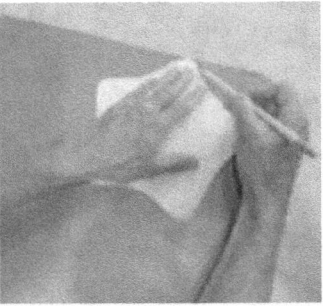

5. Use a clay knife to cut out the outline of the starfish while ensuring to incline the knife at an angle of ninety degrees to the slab. The knife will help to fetch you clean and regular cuts through the slab.

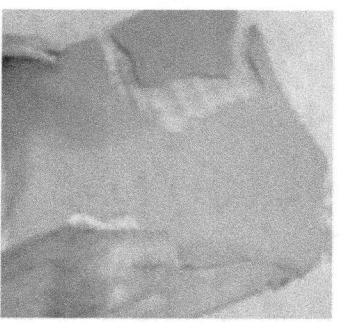

6. Set the relatively dry starfish slab over a hump-shaped mold.

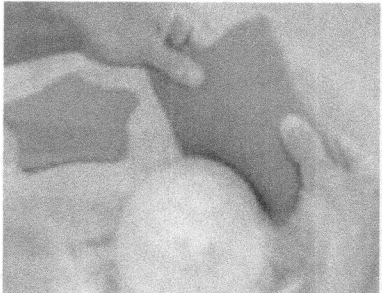

7. Press the slab to the sides of the hump.

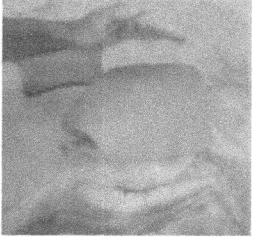

8. Shift the slab to a hump that is smaller than the initial one.

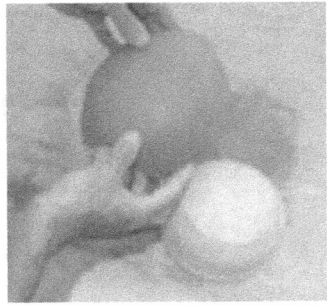

9. Press the slab to the sides of the smaller hump.

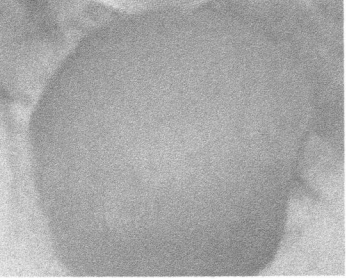

10. Star to accentuate the arms of the starfish.

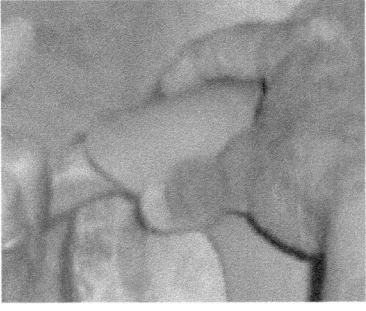

11. Do the procedure above for the rest of the arms.

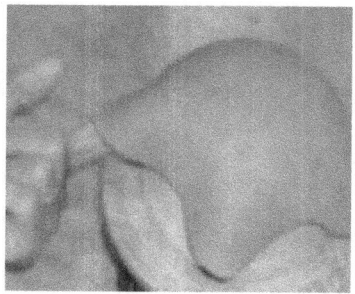

12. Lift the molded clay slab from the hump mold.

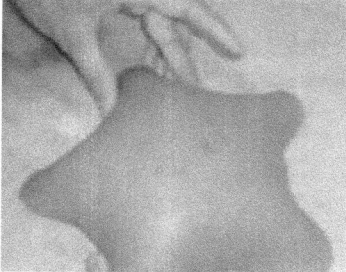

13. Make out another of the result you got in step 12 by repeating steps 1 to 12.

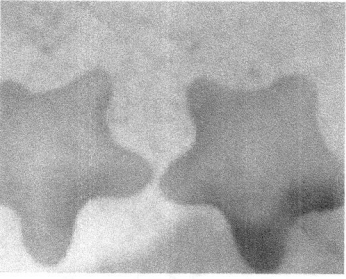

14. Use a smaller wooden cylinder to flatten the folded and molded edges.

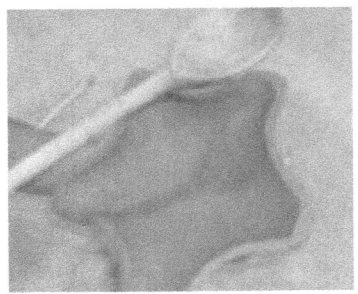

15. The slab for the starfish should look like the ones illustrated below.

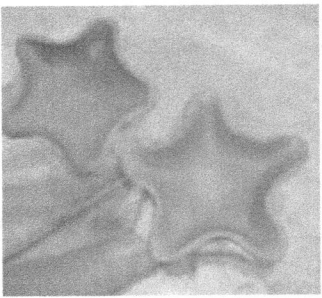

16. Score the edges of the two-star fish slabs.

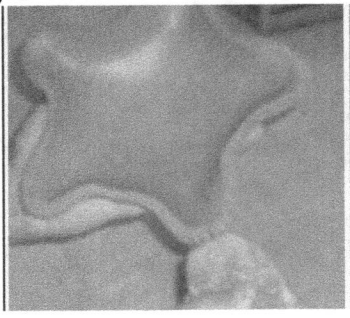

17. Add slip generously to the edges of the slabs.

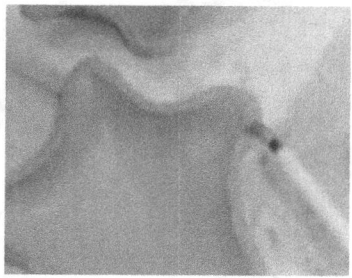

18. Press the two slabs against each other along the slipped edges.

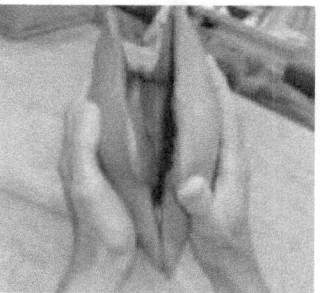

19. Blend the edges of the two starfish slabs by running your fingers along their separate ridges.

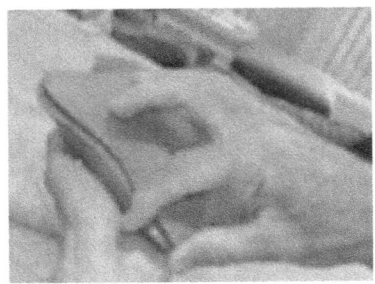

20. Roll a clay lump into a coil by rolling it across a wooden board with a little pressure.

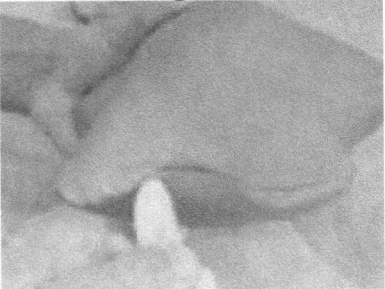

21. Press another wooden plank against the coil to get it flattened.

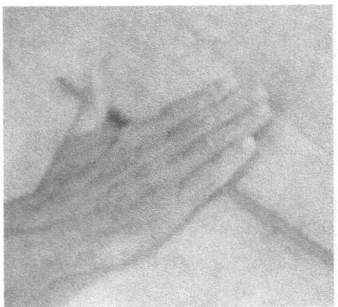

22. Set the flattened coil against the edges of contact.

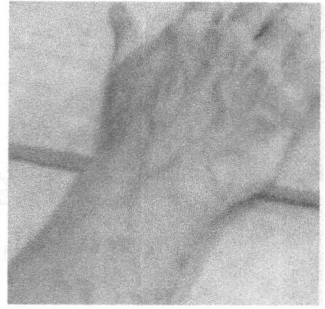

23. If you feel that the joints need to be reinforced, you could decide to add more coils of clay.

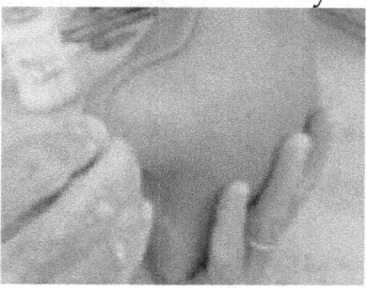

24. Run the pad of your fingers across the joints so that they are nicely blended.

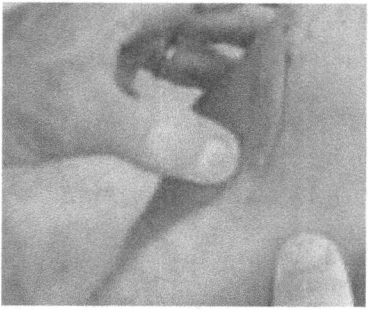

25. Use a wooden rib to make the blended edges smooth.

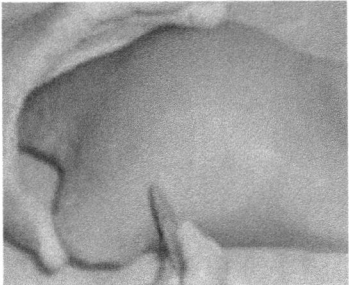

26. Run the side of a sponge across the blended joints to make it even smoother and regular.

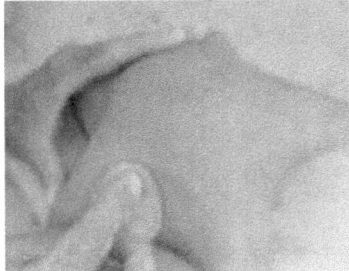

27. Define the arms by running a sponge across the edges.

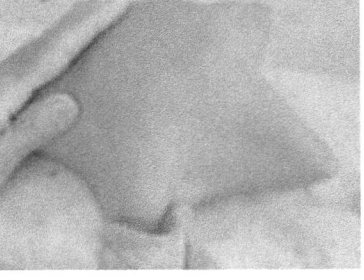

28. Now, you are done with the shape of the starfish. Your result should look something like the one illustrated below.

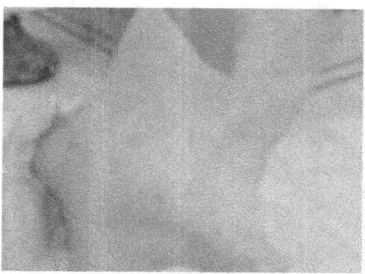

29. Mold out extensions for the arm of the starfish.

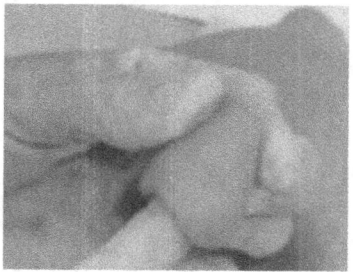

30. Run a scoring tool across the edges of the arms.

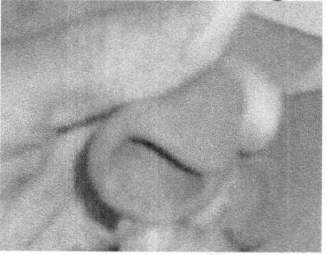

31. Use a pinning tool through the arms to allow for air passage during drying and firing. In the absence of holes, it is likely to crack or break.

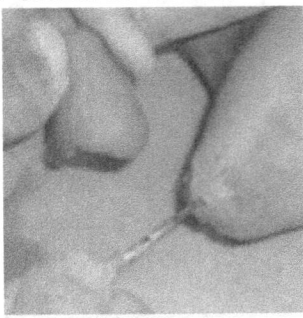

32. Add the extensions for the arm to the original extension.

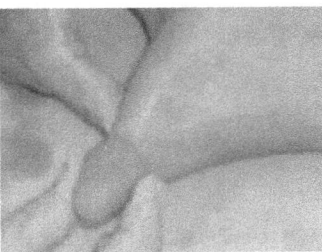

33. Fuse the extensions to the original arm by running a wooden palette across the joints.

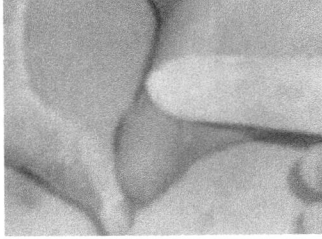

34. To reinforce the joints, you could add a coil.

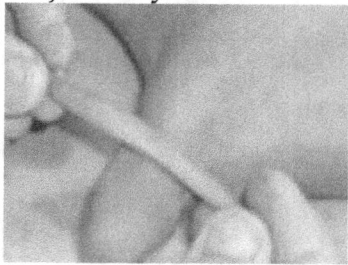

35. Now, have the coil blended with the walls of the arms.

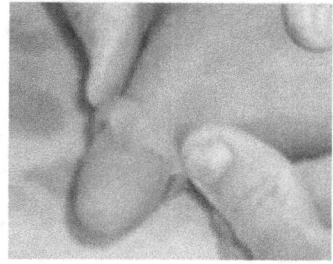

36. Adjust the arms of the starfish stylishly. The illustration below is a perfect example of stylishly designed arms.

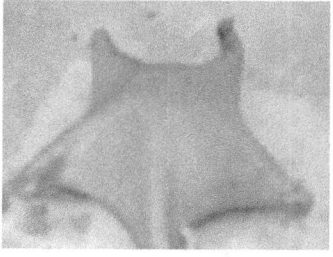

37. Use a wooden tool with a pointed edge to make outlines across the edges of the starfish.

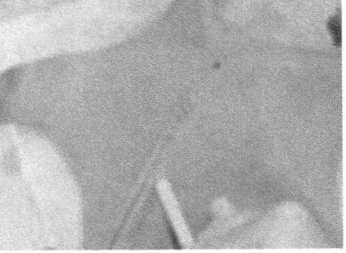

38. Fuse texture to your project by adding more lines, just like the illustration below depicts.

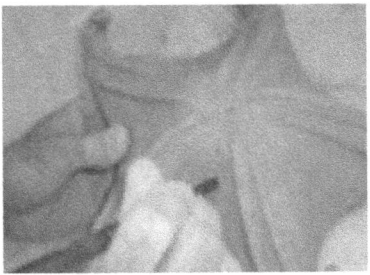

39. Add small clay lumps to the bottom of the starfish's body to create the feet.

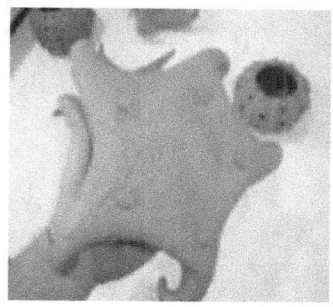

40. Then dry and fire in a kiln. The finished starfish should look like the one below. You can likewise make a lid for it.

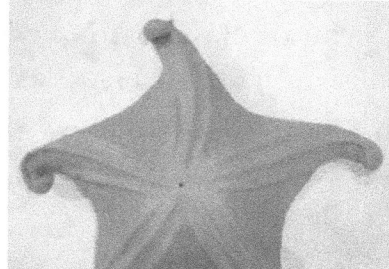
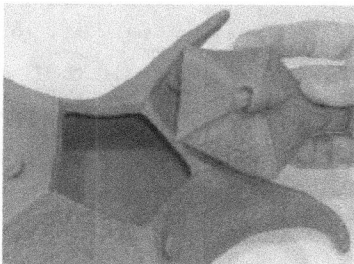

Chapter 7

Common Pottery Making Mistakes To Avoid

There are several mistakes that a beginner potter is likely to make when crafting pottery projects. Some of them are mistakes even an expert makes, so don't feel disappointed when you make mistakes in your pottery craft. However, we will discuss some of such mistakes to help you avoid them altogether.

1. Working with the wrong kind of clay: Different kinds of clay used to make pottery, and each type has its specifications and requirements. For example, some cannot be fired beyond specific temperatures, and some can. Most of these factors will, in the end, decide the final outlook of your pottery.

Porcelain, for example, is a type of clay that is known for being able to take in water quickly. It also has the consistency of butter when it is moist, and when you finish using it for your project, it would have a very regular outer surface.

Earthenware, another type of clay, is the best choice for throwing, and when it has to be fired, you don't have to work at high heat. Earthenware is the most commonly used clay.

The stoneware is popular for being able to stand the test of time. It is also a clay type that is tamper-proof. It is used for making several pottery projects, and once the projects are glazed, they might not need to be fired again.

2. Placing your arm and body wrongly while working: Placing your upper body rightly will go a long way in helping you ensure that you exert the right amount of force on anything you are working on or wedging. That way, you can also be sure that the weight is evenly distributed about the structure. Sitting in the wrong way can cause your project to be tampered with, and so, as a beginner, you must place a lot of priority on getting your body positioned in the right manner and angle.

3. Firing at low temperatures: Sometimes, the temperature that a firing process is carried out at may not be adequate to get your clay projects ready for glazing or as a white clay body. This usually occurs when the right temperature is not known. Now, before you begin to fire your clay projects, ensure to take not of the following;
- Have your pottery fired in kilns to allow you the freedom to alter the working temperature
- If you find out that it's still wet after firing pottery in the kiln, you should return the piece to the kiln. Once it is back, work at a higher temperature.
- Your kiln should be sited within a largely spaced room so that you can cancel out the risk of accidents.

4. Working with a lump of clay that offers too much resistance when it is being worked upon: The kind of clay lumps thrown on wheels is the soft kind, as it is highly needed to stick right to the surface. Clay lumps usually grow hard when you expose them to air for a long time without having a protective sheath around them. Moisture that is trapped within clay lumps can be prevented from vanishing by having them placed in damp rooms or by placing moist towels over them.

When you work with hard clay on your throwing wheel, you end up being unable to work on it or push up the walls.

5. Destruction of pottery as you pull the walls upwards: Pottery can get destroyed in a case where the structure is too weak to stand on its own. The weakness of a clay structure can occur due to unequal forces being exerted on the walls by the fingers. Excess moisture in the clay walls could also cause them to grow weak and then collapse. So, what you need to do is ensure that you avoid the materialization of such scenarios.

6. Opening a clay body too quickly: The faster you open up a clay body, the more holes you'd risk having in the final project. So, you should take your time before

proceeding to continue work on it. You could also try to moisten your fingers before you open up the clay. Another tip is to set the pad of your thumb right at the middle of the clay body.

7. Working the turning wheel at the wrong speed: The speed at which you work your throwing wheel determines how much pressure you can exact on a clay lump. The faster it moves, the lesser work you can do on the clay lump and vice versa. But then, it is best if you worked at the intermediate speed. When the wheel is moving too slowly, you end up not regulating the centering procedure, as the clay does the moving, and not your hands. When the wheel is moving too quickly, you'd hardly be able to mold a cylinder. What you'd get is something that would be very similar to a bowl.

8. Adding the wrong quantity of water to your clay: The more water you add to a clay body, the damper it becomes. You have to ensure that in all, you add just the right amount of water. Too much water will get your clay project crumbling, and a too dry project will only present issues while being molded or trimmed.

9. Wedging your clay lump wrongly: The process of wedging clay happens to be the first step to be taken

before the real art of pottery begins. Several people skip this step and begin working with the clay lump right away on the wheel. When you fail to go through with this step, what happens is that air bubbles develop within the clay and can cause hazards when it is fired within a kiln. That kind of clay is also usually hard to work on.

The end... almost!

Hey! We've made it to the final chapter of this book, and I hope you've enjoyed it so far.

If you have not done so yet, I would be incredibly thankful if you could take just a minute to leave a quick review on Amazon

Reviews are not easy to come by, and as an independent author with a little marketing budget, I rely on you, my readers, to leave a short review on Amazon.

Even if it is just a sentence or two!

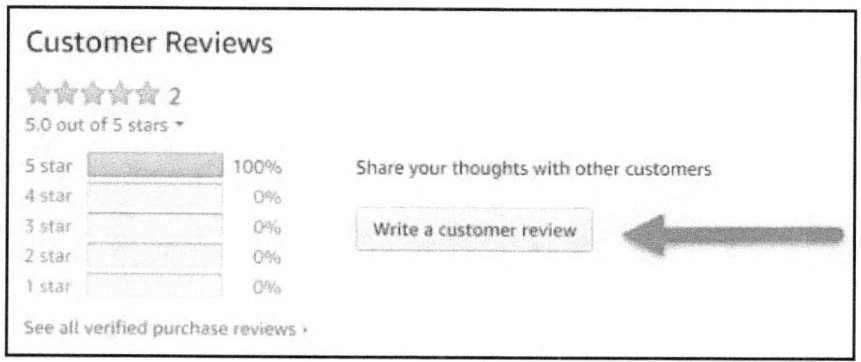

So if you really enjoyed this book, please...

\>\> Click here to leave a brief review on Amazon.

I truly appreciate your effort to leave your review, as it truly makes a huge difference.

Chapter 8

Pottery Questions To Ask Before Starting Out

Before setting out to becoming a potter, it is imperative to answer a couple of questions to aid your decision-making process. Some of these questions are provided below.

1. Are you making your pottery an ornate item or a functional one? Whatever answer you choose here is what determines the answer that you'd provide to the following other questions.

- The number of times you would need to have your project fired.
- The glazing materials you'd need in the course of the project.
- Whether or not the project is to be used or left somewhere.

Answering these questions will help prevent a scenario where you cannot use your work for anything. It is also important that you ask yourself the following questions once you have made your choice.

- Whether or not your project will have an actual use.
- Whether it will be better if you left it somewhere as a decorative piece.
- Whether or not the project is in a place where it can be broken.

2. How sharp are the edges of your project? Now, you may begin to wonder what effect sharp edges play in the decisions you make. Below are the effects that sharp-rimmed pottery can have.

- You could end up cutting across your skin with it.
- You wouldn't be able to use it as a drinking tool.

The issue with this question is that you wouldn't be able to enjoy using cups with sharp handles.

3. Do you plan on firing your project in a kiln or an oven? If you are going to consider firing your project in a kiln, you might want to consider the following;
- The cost of installing and running a kiln.
- Kilns can fetch more heat and indifferent extents too.
- Many clay projects can be fired within a kiln.

- Kilns can help to make your glazing materials stick to the body of your project.
- If you are going to work with a kiln, you would need technical know-how.

Also, if you plan on working with an oven, the following factors should be considered;

- The time the oven will take to get the project completely fired.
- Using an oven is a wonderful firing method for beginners
- The result you get here doesn't come out to be as strong as the one you get from a kiln.
- There are more stringent rules attached to the use of an oven.
- Ovens cannot fire bisque projects.
- Ovens can only be good for you if you plan on making ornate pieces.

4. Can my kiln handle the clay and glazes temperatures?

- Earthenware, for example, can be fired at temperatures as low as 1500-degrees.
- For stoneware, the temperature gets even higher, about 2200-degrees.

- For porcelain, you'd need to fire at a temperature as high as 355-degrees.

So, you would need to know the firing capacity of your kiln to determine if it'd be able to facilitate your project. For example, the dental kilns are only capable of firing the porcelain kind of clay slightly.

So, it is best for only earthenware and stoneware. Now, moving on to the topic of glazing, you might need to consider the following factors;

- Bisque projects go through two firing processes.
- Each of the processes lasts for about ten to twelve hours.
- While glazing, you'd need to be around to supervise the firing.
- You'd need to work at a temperature that is just suitable for the glazing material.

5. Are you going to be constructing your pottery with your hand or with the aid of a wheel? Both options have their good and bad sides, and here, we will discuss them.

Building a pottery project with your hands is feasible for the following projects.

- Jars and other projects can be built on slabs.
- Jars and other projects can be built with coils.
- Bowls and other projects can be built with the pinch method.

Now, we'd discuss why the hand-building technique could work just fine and why it may not.

- It is cheap.
- It does not require technical know-how.
- You can do many projects with this technique. It's more for beginners.
- It is mostly designed for ornate pieces.
- Projects built with this technique are usually not symmetrical.

Pottery wheels are excellent choices because you can make virtually everything you need—pots, cups, vessels, anything. The good sides and bad sides of this choice will also be discussed below;

- You have to get a throwing wheel to start with.
- If you choose to operate on wheels that are manually pedaled, you could end up getting fatigued.
- Pottery wheels help your projects to be symmetrical.

- It helps the supposedly round projects to be round.

6. Are you going to wedge your clay or get it supplied to you in usable forms? The advantages of purchasing the clay you need include the following;

- You would be able to work with the exact dimensions since the clay would have been measured.
- You can get the clay in large quantities.
- It's very good for spontaneous preparations.

The advantages of making your clay include the following;

- It is a cheaper option.
- You can alter a couple of recipes if you like.
- You could whip up something different from the available rest.
- You get to spoon in some added features to your clay.
- It can be very simple to do.

7. How big do you want your handles to be? This question has to do with the function that your pottery is

playing. Now, if the vessel is to contain hot liquids, you'd want to insulate the handle. Handles that are too big usually would cause a few of these problems;

- It is usually quite heavy.
- You wouldn't find it easy to use such a project.

And now, if the handles are too small;

- They would be more susceptible to breakage.
- You wouldn't be able to hold them comfortably.
- You could somehow drop it while working with it.

8. Do you feel you will work faster if you open your kiln up? If you are going to open up your kiln at all, you have to do it slowly, as the following issues could occur;

- Cracking under the force of it all.
- Crazing of the pottery.
- Shattering of the pottery.

The kiln should also not be hot for that to be successful. Now, why would you even want to open your kiln?

- You could open it if you need the crack lines on your pottery.

- If you want it to cool down a lot sooner.
- If you need to have it painted.

9. Can mistakes be fixed? If your bisque project has an issue, you could fix it by doing the following;

- Running a damp sponge across the surface.
- Getting it back on the wheel for more work.

For already fired projects, the following tips could pay off;

- Sanding the pottery.
- Glazing and firing the pottery again.
- Glazing your project.

Also, if you find yourself susceptible to making errors, you could do any of the following;

- Work only on projects that correspond with your skills.
- Ensure that you know the nitty-gritty of a project before trying it out.
- Fixing your errors before firing them.
- Learn from your other mistakes.
- Rub off any marks you might have left on the pottery.

I wish you all the best!

Happy Molding, Potters!!!

www.ingramcontent.com/pod-product-compliance
Lightning Source LLC
Chambersburg PA
CBHW071413070526
44578CB00003B/568